Municipal

Executive Policy Governance

GEORGE B. CUFF

brought to you by the publishers of

Municipal World
CANADA'S MUNICIPAL MAGAZINE

2014

©Municipal World Inc., 2014

All rights reserved. No part of this publication may be reproduced, stored in a retrieval system, or transmitted, in any form or by any means, photocopying, electronic, mechanical recording, or otherwise, without the prior written permission of the copyright holder.

Library and Archives Canada Cataloguing in Publication

Cuff, George B., author

    Executive policy governance : a leadership model for local government / George B. Cuff.

(Municipal knowledge series)

ISBN 978-1-926843-06-3 (pbk.)

    1. Political leadership. 2. Municipal officials and employees. 3. Municipal government. 4. Public administration. I. Title. II. Series: Municipal knowledge series

JF1525.L4C83 2014   352.23'62   C2014-903887-9

Published in Canada by
Municipal World Inc.
42860 Sparta Line
Union, Ontario N0L 2L0
2014
mwadmin@municipalworld.com
www.municipalworld.com

ITEM 0056

Municipal World — Reg. T.M. in Canada Municipal World Inc.

TABLE OF CONTENTS

	Foreword v
Chapter 1	Released to Lead 1
Chapter 2	What Does a Council Do?. 5
Chapter 3	The Monkey Wrench 21
Chapter 4	10 Principles of Good Governance for Effective Councils. 27
Chapter 5	Impact of the Chosen Governance Model . . . 35
Chapter 6	Common Governance Models 45
Chapter 7	Case for a New Model: Executive Policy Governance. 57
Chapter 8	Foundational Principles and Design Criteria . . 69
Chapter 9	Understanding Executive Policy Governance. . 79
Chapter 10	Taking Action within a Decision-Making Framework 93
Chapter 11	Establishing a Policy Framework 103
Chapter 12	Developing a Policy Mindset 109
Chapter 13	Importance of Council Meetings 117
Chapter 14	Impact of the Mayor. 121

Chapter 15	Role of Standing Committees and ABCs 127
Chapter 16	Impact of Administrative Advice 131
Chapter 17	Where Does the Public Fit? 135
Chapter 18	Review of Key Concepts 143
Chapter 19	Drawing the Strings Together. 147

Foreword

It is perhaps refreshing to candidly admit that all one's previous efforts have failed. While that may be an exaggeration, the fact remains that, after 35 years of consulting in and to the public sector, the evidence is stark and disturbing: those leading organizations because they have been either elected or appointed do not often seem to "get it."

Leadership is not merely attending meetings of council or various boards. Leadership is not simply passing resolutions on the recommendation of the senior staff member, or approving the minutes of an advisory body. Leadership is not engaging in heated debate to the point of causing offence because this or that fellow council member does not agree to your obviously superior and well-reasoned solution. Unfortunately, however, that is exactly how it seems to be understood by some. I would even argue that we have had people in elected office who have diligently served for two or three decades and who have still not figured out how to lead!

Leadership is a scarce and very valuable commodity that is absolutely critical to the success or failure of organizations. It is often more known by its absence than its presence. Leaders influence others to move in a particular direction. They can often see a target more clearly and more quickly than others; and, they have the presence necessary to cause others to move (or desire to move) in that direction. Leadership is the art of getting others to the preferred destination.

This book is intended to be useful to those elected to serve at the local level – in any system that is based on democratic principles.

Those principles include voting rights, equity, fairness, respect for the rule of law, and a willingness to adhere to democratically-determined decisions. It is not a primer, nor is it an academic treatise. It presumes a basic understanding of the principles of good governance and a recognition of the high value placed upon the administrative leaders who often serve at the pleasure of elected leaders.

These principles and practices work. They are sound and functional, and they cross the borders of large and small local government organizations (and many related agencies), rural and urban. I would argue that the principles work equally well in locally elected school boards and, with some tweaking, in other public sector agencies as well. It is my hope that you find this to be so.

I am thankful for my career in local government specifically, and in consulting generally. My role as an advisor, an elected official, and a teacher of sound governance has afforded me countless opportunities to meet new people who are trying to make a difference in the lives of others.

My work over the years has been very time- and energy-consuming. Supporting me through this journey (with all of its bumps along the way) has been my wife, Arliss. I am thankful to God for her.

George B. Cuff, FCMC

2014

A personal note: As with my royalties from other books I have written, the proceeds of this book will go towards supporting Falcon Rock Camp for children in a very disadvantaged part of our world, northwestern Romania. Thank you for your contribution to this important cause.

Chapter 1
Released to Lead

The key flaw in how municipal councils function, in my opinion, lies quite clearly in the method of governance. That is, if councils are to govern effectively, they must be "released to lead." The value that a council brings to the table is not the combined expertise of all members of an elected council; rather, it is that council's capacity to actually lead the community towards its preferred future. How it does this task is the key to whether or not it will be successful.

Considerable time is spent on council decision making; but often, (though not always), the focus is placed on how council can be more efficient with its use of time, as opposed to how council can be more effective. Historically, we have succeeded in "boxing in" councils by establishing the parameters as to what issues they are allowed to address. This has been accomplished through the laws governing municipalities and their allied agencies (including school boards) and by the powers granted through the local government charters that have become more in vogue in certain jurisdictions within North America. Councils have, however, struggled with identifying what *their* central, defining role is and how they can add real value to their communities in the decision-making process.

In the Beginning

I begin with the perspective that the folks elected to local governments or appointed to their many off-shoots begin with a strong desire to lead and to add value to their respective communities. They want their time to count. They are not interested in simply warming the chair or having a title. They are compelled by the quaint notion that, if you want to improve something, you need to have demonstrated your personal commitment. While many newly-elected folks may not fully appreciate what they are to do (compared to those who are actually employed by the municipality), they at least approach the "job" with a keenness that is hard to escape. They want to see their municipality, town, or village stay as "healthy" as it is and, if possible, become better. They often want to help create or nurture an environment in which their children and grandchildren can grow their families, get a good education, play, and work.

In many instances, however, there is little interest in examining how best to utilize the time, input, and gifts of those governing so as to better the future of our communities. Municipalities are creative in many ways and are often open to changing the way they carry out what they see as their "primary tasks." They are resilient: they take on increasing obligations due to legislative changes that place the burden for services on them. Municipalities have not, however, spent much time or effort in examining what seems to be expected of them as governing bodies; and thus, how they get the job done is largely a reflection of how it was done by the last group of councillors (a term used here to include both board members and aldermen).

In some ways, we seem to have ascribed the "big picture / broad vision" core of governing to other levels of government, while local governments are expected to focus on the actual day-to-day tasks of public service delivery. Unfortunately, in some instances at least, local governments have become aligned with the notion of being "closest to the people" – without really thinking through what that means in terms of governing their affairs, as opposed to helping citizens manage their lives.

Those elected to local councils (and related governing bodies such as regional districts and school boards) are expected to demonstrate leadership. They are presumed to be people who think broadly – people who see things with a breadth of vision that escapes the mindset of ordinary citizens. While each elected official needs to understand and relate to the "here and now," they also must recognize that much of their real value as a composite body is the ability to see beyond – to be released to lead. When councils are stuck in the mire of only the immediate, they fail to take advantage of real opportunities to effect significant change. Leaders are not content to rest on the status quo. They want what's better for their fellow citizens. Status quo is for those who cannot or who will not think creatively, who always ask the question: "Who else does things this way?"

What's Missing?

So, what is missing? I would argue that local governments have not made good use of the primary roles (and thus value) of their elected leaders. For far too long, they have seen members of council as extensions of the administration (cheap extensions mind you, but extensions nonetheless). Neither council members nor their senior administrations have taken the time or extra effort to determine what is the best thing the council could do, as opposed to "How do we fill in another council agenda?" It is not that some of the issues on the agenda are not important, or perhaps even required. However, the imperative to fill the agenda leaves little time for council to reflect on what strategic input would be really useful to the community at the present time – to consider whether they are leaders or maintainers.

This book is focused on how councils should govern – not manage. It is an attempt to address the issue of how each council can maximize its impact on its respective community and provide the leadership that residents both want and need. It is an essential text for elected and appointed officials alike if local governments are to move beyond the world of "pipes and pavement." It is for those who understand that citizens both desire and need leaders with vision and big dreams to lead their precious communities.

Chapter 2
What Does a Council Do?

The key theme of this book addresses the need for improved policy governance. It is not a manual on what the legislation says is permissible in your jurisdiction. I am aware that there are many variations in the legislation for local governments across North America; but, having given seminars on both sides of the border, I am also aware that there are significant commonalities as well. It is with the latter in mind that I write. It is hoped that nothing in the following materials will cause confusion. Questions about the application of anything written herein could be resolved by reference to an experienced municipal lawyer or perhaps a legislative consultant in your jurisdiction.

General Responsibilities

Each municipal council has basic, generic responsibilities that flow from legislation, including local charters and by-laws. These responsibilities, while not necessarily common in their interpretation across jurisdictions, are focused on the basic services necessary to the ongoing ability of a local government to function. These include the following:

- ➤ Safety and security
  - provision of policing services
  - enforcement of by-laws
  - provision of fire protection services
- ➤ Delivery of utility services
  - water treatment and distribution

- sewage treatment and disposal
- power (electrical/gas) services

➤ Preservation of public assets
- maintenance of roadways
- maintenance of park spaces
- maintenance of public facilities

➤ Provision of leisure services
- delivery of recreation programs
- delivery of cultural programs

➤ Provision of municipal planning and building services
- development of a general municipal plan
- identification of future land uses/growth patterns/open spaces
- coordination of building inspection services

➤ Provision of social services
- coordination of public health services
- provision of services to the disadvantaged
- delivery of social / affordable housing

➤ Promotion of the community
- identification of community image
- promotion of economic development opportunities
- development of a community website or branding identity
- identification of tourism options and obstacles
- connection to council and administration

These broadly described "service envelopes" are considered critical to the sustainable continuance of civic functions. While not all are considered local responsibilities by all jurisdictions, they represent the core of any healthy community. Some jurisdictions are more extensively regulated, while others have such services provided by other orders of government.

What Role Does a Council Have?

Each council has a leadership role relative to these services. Each council must determine the level of service provided, and thus, the degree of funding such services will require. This determination lies at the heart of civic budgets and drives tax rates and utility charges. Such decisions are not made in isolation: they are considered in light of what the council deems to be priorities, both in terms of their urgency, as well as overall importance to the community.

Leadership

It falls to each council to guide the community according to what elected officials see as being needed or desired by a majority of citizens. This requires the collective wisdom of council, supported by the advice of the administration. The *way* in which a council governs (that is, makes decisions) may differ quite substantially from community to community, but the need to govern is apparent to all.

Where issues are either substantive or likely to be repetitive, council may need to consider what policy stance would make the most sense and be most likely to ensure an appropriate and timely response in the future. Policy governance (a theme I will be developing throughout this book) requires that council be alert to issues of concern to citizens, including those that they may have already raised with a previous elected council. Such issues require council to give its full attention to how such matters can be resolved and to consider whether or not a well-reasoned policy can be (or already has been) articulated.

Leadership requires the ability to judge issues and requests on their merits and to resolve differences. Sometimes, those differences lie between two neighbours, while at other times they may impact subdivisions. Council members need to determine whether or not development should proceed in a particular area of the community and, if so, to what density. Councils are regularly challenged to sort out "the greater good" sought by a group of residents and their legitimate concerns, relative to the best interests of the municipality as a whole.

As a part of this leadership role, there is an expectation by citizens that council will seek to provide good government. However, providing "good" government is not a simple task. It is the sum total of all that a council does, which ranges from the mundane of approving minutes and correspondence, to the more complex world of rezoning and long-range planning. Each council's decisions are predicated on answering one basic question: What is in the best interests of our residents and businesses now and into the foreseeable future? Good government reflects all of a council's efforts to resolve such a question in a common sense, decent, compassionate manner.

There are a number of obvious barriers in the way, including:

- the inadequacies of communicating to the population as a whole the wide range of issues that council will encounter during any term of office;
- the impact of key issues and the pressure to make clear-headed decisions on a multitude of such issues; and
- the fact that the municipality may be comprised of wards, and the resulting focus by councillors on what best serves their particular wards, as opposed to what best serves the municipality as a whole (this is contrary to the legislation, which generally stresses the interests of the whole).

The drafters of legislation would have understood these challenges and recognized that any council would face such barriers. There is, however, the underlying presumption that men and women of goodwill will purposely set about to act in a manner that would seek the best for their citizens, based on what each individually and collectively saw as the appropriate course of action. This requires us to have confidence in the sincerity and commitment of each member to serve in an honest fashion, whatever the "best interests" of the public are felt to be. Further, it presumes that each member will pay heed to other colleagues on council and sift through the arguments to see the basis upon which the position is being put forward.

Authorize, fund, and deliver services

While some services may be required of a municipality by other orders of government, council must often make choices with respect

Chapter 2 • What Does a Council Do? 9

to other services requested, but not previously budgeted. In some jurisdictions, that may entail social (or affordable) housing, while in others the challenge may be to take the lead role in dealing with local poverty.

Much of what any council does is legislated by the province. According to various pieces of legislation guiding municipalities across Canada, the council may (or in some cases must):

- regulate public utilities;
- regulate public thoroughfares, including highways and road allowances;
- establish regulations governing use of private property, including businesses;
- provide access to a public sewage utility;
- keep highways and bridges in a good state of repair;
- cause decayed trees to be removed if they are perceived to constitute a danger;
- establish a passenger transportation system;
- regulate waste;
- provide for culture, parks, and recreation services;
- acquire, maintain, and/or add to heritage facilities and regulate same;
- regulate animal control and other public nuisances;
- fund economic and community development activities;
- fund municipal capital facilities;
- regulate smoking in public and in workplaces;
- establish a communication system for emergency response purposes;
- regulate signage;
- establish procedures governing council and committee meetings; and
- pay salaries to staff and provide pensions and other benefits.

The range of both permitted and required duties of council is significant. There is little that happens in any community that is not impacted by the powers of council. Such powers obviously need to be exercised judiciously and with due care, such that the rights of both the perceived majority and minority are respected.

Council may also be expected to negotiate with a neighbouring jurisdiction for the purpose of combining resources so that recreation facilities are open to all citizens of both communities. This will often require elected officials to act in a more collaborative fashion, so that questions of ownership or location are superseded by what is in the best interests of the larger population.

Policies and budgets frequently determine service levels. Does the municipality grade snow or water lawns at this interval or that? Are public facilities open for use at 6 a.m. or 7 a.m.? Such questions are generally determined by council or an administrative corporate policy (which is often dependent upon the local ability to fund). Many policy decisions – particularly relating to service levels – are directly impacted by approved budget resources. That decision, in turn, is generally made or approved by the local council.

Whenever councils are considering how to fine-tune their budgets to meet unexpected challenges, they examine choices. While there may be small projects that can be temporarily shelved, any significant budgetary change will likely require that other services be suspended or dropped, or the level of service cut. None of those choices are without a degree of pain. Every project has supporters in the community.

Represent the community as a whole

Legislation across Canada directs councils to be concerned with the well-being of the public from a "community as a whole" point of view. That is, members of council should be prepared to give equal weight to opinions and input gathered from all quarters (or wards/divisions) of the municipality, and not over-emphasize those from a particular vested interest or from a specific area of the municipality. It is a challenge (particularly in rural areas or large cities, both of which generally function within a "ward" model of government) to appreciate how good decisions for the greater good will "spill over" to encompass all regions.

While it may be argued that a particular issue affects one group more so than another, the collective opinion of council may be that the municipality also profits from the decision. For example, restoring a historic structure may be advocated by the historical society, and thus, they may be the first to applaud a positive decision by council ... but, the overall good of the community is also positively impacted by the addition of a resource that brings in increased tourism or one that enhances the range of services the municipality is able to offer.

As another example, the construction of a major arena may result in significant cost to all taxpayers, and may initially be perceived as only benefiting either the private sector owner or a particular sports group. In the final analysis, however, there will likely be a tremendous advantage to all citizens through the addition of a first-rate entertainment complex that enhances the viability of the community as a whole, in addition to restoring a healthy tax base in the area abutting the facility.

Communicate with the public

Members of council are expected to maintain an ongoing relationship with the public through both informal and formal means of communication. Informed communication reflects more of an implicit understanding between the community and its elected council. Formal communication may be required on certain projects, or when seeking community approval in order to pass the borrowing by-law for a capital project.

It is a source of both irony and cynicism that those elected on the basis of being good communicators often fail to maintain even limited contact with the public after being elected. There is simply an enticement to private decision making that cannot be relied upon to garner the support of the public. While decisions discussed in private might seem to be more free-flowing and comprehensive, they are not transparent, and *transparency* is what the public expects.

One of council's primary responsibilities is to communicate its plans to its citizens. While this is done in numerous ways (and in limited ways by some), each council relies upon the support that it is able to garner and sustain from its publics. Where an issue is deemed to be quite significant, then council should find ways to ensure that the public is not only made aware of the issue to be resolved, but also informed about how they can get involved in the decision-making process.

In some instances, a council member might be contacted by a member of the public with respect to an issue that he or she has been unable to have satisfactorily resolved. Having been so notified, the council member has an obligation to ensure that the administration has also been made aware of the issue and how to contact the person making the inquiry or filing the complaint.

In today's environment, with a much greater array of communication forums, attention needs to be paid to how your citizens connect with council and "town hall." In some instances, that connection is electronic; in others, and certainly for a community with a largely older population, more attention will need to be paid to "high touch" communication, rather than "high tech."

Set priorities

Councils also have the distinct challenge of identifying what services or programs are considered to be absolute priorities by the public. This is not a simple task, given that such decisions can vary from term to term, and can in fact be varied within a term of office.

This role requires council to not only listen carefully to what the administration is advising, but to also "hear" what the community is saying. The challenge is not simple: it might require a year-long process of meeting with various groups or agencies; or it may result in council spending the funds necessary to retain external expertise to ensure that all voices are being heard.

It is frustrating in the extreme to see council go through such a deliberate process, only to have the results readily set aside as soon as a delegation suggests working on some other initiative immediately. Or, to realize that the weekend retreat devoted to setting goals could be so quickly forgotten or even ignored.

Councils need to understand that, while they may have to face emerging issues as they arise, their focus must be placed on those issues and policies that have the potential to bring about the greatest good for the community as a whole, over a reasonable time frame. Is that so difficult to understand or to expect?

Fiduciary leadership

Council has a responsibility to the community in providing assurance that the financial and organizational resources are in decent shape. This assumes that council will guide business/strategic planning, as well as the budget approval process, in order to assure prudent oversight relative to fiscal clarity and reporting. Again, this does not presume that members of council need to be well versed in municipal accounting in order to be effective; rather, it suggests that all members are obligated to assure themselves that the actions of the administration are in keeping with the policies and approvals of council.

Council should, at a minimum, hold an annual meeting with its external auditor to request assurance that the municipal corporation is functioning as expected and in accordance with generally acceptable municipal accounting principles. Council should receive a confidential briefing by the external auditor as to the financial stability of the organization, together with a review of the internal controls, investment policies, variance reporting, and financial management policies and practices. Council should then meet with the CAO and chief financial officer and determine how and when they will be briefed by the CAO and CFO as to compliance with the recommendations of the auditor.

Initiate policies and programs

Leadership requires that leaders lead. This requires the expression of initiative and a desire to not only improve what the municipality is currently doing, but to challenge whether it should be done at all. In many instances, there seems to be a reliance on previous councils' judgments, as though they must have "got it right," when, in fact, that may not have been the case.

Council is expected to participate generally in developing and evaluating the policies and programs of the municipality. Thus, while the CAO is generally responsible for recommending policies and programs to council, it is up to the elected officials to determine what is in the best interests of residents and what can be realistically incorporated into the municipal budget. It is also incumbent upon elected officials to determine if the municipality actually has real policies, or is simply accustomed to doing things a certain way. Any debate in council that goes past the 10-minute mark should be interrupted by someone who queries, "What's our policy respecting this issue?" It should not be surprising (by the end of a meandering 10 munutes) to find that there is none, or that it has not been referenced in some time and needs to be refreshed.

It is important that council evaluate the present policies and programs to ensure that they are still relevant, and that they are providing the results that council initially intended.

Participate in meetings

In order to discharge these duties fairly and responsibly, all members of council are expected to take an active role in council meetings. This is where key decisions should be made, and where council's role as the final arbiter of matters within their jurisdiction is played out. This does not necessitate that members be equally involved in terms of "air time," but rather, that they are *entitled* to be equally involved. Most will listen to the key points being put forward by their colleagues and make their own determination as to the merits of the arguments. In some instances, the arguments may be sufficient to influence their vote on the issues; in other cases, however, prior review of background material and contacts during the week with other committee members and the administration may have provided sufficient support for an alternate course of action.

Participating in meetings presumes certain preconditions:

- all members are willing to respect the input offered by their colleagues;
- all members have actually reviewed the agenda package in advance and are prepared to debate the issues intelligently or at least from a perspective of being informed; and
- all members have kept their minds open, so that the debate and input actually means something.

Represent council at meetings of ABCs

As we continue in this section on "What Does a Council Do?" it is important to note the potential impact that council members' attendance at meetings of agencies, boards, and committees (ABCs) can have on the decision-making process. These internal and external bodies actually carry considerable weight (or at least have the potential for doing so), and can influence council decisions.

While we will examine this matter more closely in the material that follows, it is safe to say that most (if not all) councils have a range of ABCs that they are expected to meet with on either a regular or perhaps infrequent basis. The bulk of such groups and organizations are important in any community. They offer a service to their fellow residents in terms of their mandate by providing focus to their issues and by offering programs and services to their community. They might take the form of a historical society, library board, Communities in Bloom committee, airport society, recreation board, or many other such groups.

The role of members of council on such boards and committees needs to be clearly evaluated and identified. Members of council are not expected to be advocates for this or that body; rather, it is their role to act as a liaison on behalf of council. This enables council members to reserve their judgment on the key issues until such time as they have heard from other members of council, and have also received expert commentary from the administration.

Determine the public acceptance of tax rates

A further local government responsibility is the determination of tax rates. This annual exercise often takes place without much informed public input and with limited opportunities for council to get a comprehensive "read" as to what the public expects or will endure.

Most communities do not have the resources to do any sophisticated or expensive polling of their citizens to see what increases would be acceptable. Few have figured out how to make the information and the options available in a digestible package for the public. While today's "connected" generation makes communication of information very quick, the nuances of the options require more time to explain. As a result, council often proceeds on the basis of what it believes to be publicly palatable.

Develop a safe and secure community

Each council has the significant obligation of determining how best to ensure that their community is safe from danger (whether manmade or by nature), such that its citizens can live peaceably and with a reasonable sense of freedom from unwanted intrusion into their space or danger to their person or property. For many citizens, the availability and rapid response of emergency personnel (fire, police, and paramedics) is number one on the list of services needed from their elected leaders. Any change to this equation can (and often is) met with hostility and considerable resistance, because the sanctity of home and personal lives are at stake.

Council also has an obligation to ensure that the prevailing laws and by-laws governing the municipality are being upheld. This requires council and all of its members (and the administration) to understand how the laws apply to their behaviour and what constitutes reasonable restrictions on their actions and decisions. This duty applies to legislation around conflict of interest and accepting pecuniary benefits, as well as by-laws regulating the number of dogs a property owner is allowed to have on any one residential property. Because council members are so much in the public eye, their actions and statements need not only be right, but also *seen* to be right. That is, the public places a higher burden of ethical behaviour on a member of council than it might on a fellow neighbour.

Citizens want to be assured that their council is doing everything possible, within the reasonable constraints of funding and staff, to ensure that they can conduct their lives in a safe and peaceful manner.

Manage and preserve the community's public assets

Every community has assets – some large, some small; some expensive, others not. These assets might include open spaces, public buildings, roadways, utility corridors, public works equipment, fire and policing equipment, historical properties, and recreational/cultural facilities. The list goes on. The local government has an obligation to ensure assets that are deemed to be publicly owned are indeed managed wisely, with an eye to the future.

Council has an obligation to keep the cost of maintaining such services in front of the public, as well as to communicate the expected downside if care and attention are not paid to both visible and underground assets. Councils miss the mark if they are not continually reminding their citizens of the need to maintain what is there: each day the infrastructure ages and, while it may not be apparent due to being largely underground, it will deteriorate unless regular maintenance is performed. Further, funds need to be set aside annually if replacement is to take place down the road without incurring a major shortfall in the budget. (This logic, of course, defies the "no increase in taxes" philosophy, which ignores the need to set aside the funds required to replace infrastructure when it is essential to do so.)

Assets will also include those individuals who work for the municipality – and such assets are even more important. Employees must be looked after, paid for their services, encouraged in their work, and directed in their performance of that work. Finding quality people to serve local governments is always important, and never more so than now as baby boomers retire and a new generation of leaders is being sought. As a result, ensuring that the current administration is properly compensated and appreciated is critical if they are to be confident in your commitment to their future employment and career progression.

The community also needs to put into place appropriate policies and systems to guard its financial resources gained from taxes, collections, and investments. These assets can run into millions of dollars, with the community as a corporate entity often being the richest "business" in town. Such resources must be secured through sound policies and control systems that will pass the scrutiny of an external auditor.

Foster current and future economic, social, and environmental well-being of municipality

Council has the responsibility to ensure that the future of the community is sustainable. Each council assumes office with hopes and aspirations for making improvements, and tries to do so by guiding the planning and budgeting of community resources. At the same time, and over-riding all other aspects, council must always be cognizant of how its decisions impact the municipality's capacity to continue functioning in a viable manner. While this may seem a point of limited value, there have been communities that could no longer be sustained through normal taxation and access to grant funds, requiring them to lower the flag and declare insolvency (or to request a merger with a larger neighbour).

The principle of sustainability or "assured succession" implies that what exists at present will be there for the foreseeable future. That is one of the requirements of any municipal organization – to ensure, to the extent possible, its continuance through effective planning and careful management of fiscal resources. This does not ignore the very real possibility that a small municipality might find it impossible to carry on. That discussion needs to involve larger neighbours with access to more resources (and likely the provincial government).

Part of being a community leader is the expectation that any actions or initiatives will only be pursued if the view of council is that such actions are in the best interests of the community. The community is where it is at today because of the prudent choices made by those in whose steps the present generation of leaders is following. Similarly, the community of tomorrow will be impacted by the actions of today's decision makers.

Deliver and participate in provincial initiatives

Municipalities are a creation of the Canadian constitution, which grants provincial governments the right to create and empower local governments. Through this arrangement, provinces have provided municipalities not only funding programs for certain kinds of service delivery, but also the requirement to implement certain services within a legislated framework. Thus, while funding might be made available for highways, they must be built to a specified standard and operated within provincially-mandated limits. Similarly, funding may be made available for particular social services, but only be accessible if those delivering the services are registered members of the social service profession. And, the legislated provisions often vary from province to province.

As long as the provincial governments retain power over municipalities, there will continue to be the need for the latter to ensure that their programs, policies, and services are not directly contrary to the policy framework of their respective province. Where the local government is granted sole authority, policies may be quite different – and may well irritate the provincial cabinet. However, where funding agreements are substantial, "biting the hand that feeds you" has not typically been a carefully thought-out strategy!

Ensure council decisions are implemented

Council is to ensure that administrative practices and procedures are in place to implement the decisions of council. Unfortunately, this duty can be understood to require council to become involved in the activities and decisions of the administration. This is not the appropriate interpretation, however. The intent, rather, is to put mechanisms in place to assure council that the CAO is actively guiding staff to properly and promptly discharge council decisions.

There is little likelihood that any council will be advised regarding all decisions being implemented – or will want to be. On the other hand, every council should be briefed as to the ongoing implementation of key policy issues via a regular update provided by the CAO. Such a "key issues dossier" could then be circulated to council on a regular basis as a means of providing an update on the status of progress on council's major issues.

Assess results

Having made decisions, resolved issues, approved business plans and budgets, issued directives, or proclaimed policies, council has one final chore: to assess results. If, and that is a big **IF**, council has established its goals and priorities at the start of the year, then it needs to close the loop with some form of evaluation at year-end. This might be in the form of a citizen satisfaction survey, a random sampling of households relative to key issues, or a series of open houses to seek honest and comprehensive public feedback.

The mayor could offer a year-end summary of goals and accomplishments and, with that, his or her "report card" on what has been achieved by this council.

If nothing else, council should meet with its administration and determine if, in their collective opinion, the community has been relatively well served. This informal process (provided it is not overly self-serving), can be a useful step towards pursuing ongoing improvement the following year.

Summary

The foregoing roles and responsibilities are significant. Council is charged with requirements that speak to the core of what citizens expect from their community leaders. Members of council are expected to:

- lead and provide good government;
- authorize, fund, and deliver services;
- represent the community as a whole;
- communicate with the public;
- set priorities;
- ensure fiduciary leadership;
- initiate policies and programs;
- participate in meetings;
- represent council at meetings of ABCs;
- determine the public's acceptance of tax rates;
- develop and maintain a safe and secure community;
- manage and preserve the public's assets;
- foster the current and future economic, social, and environmental well-being of the municipality;
- deliver and participate in provincial initiatives;
- ensure council decisions are implemented; and
- assess results.

Chapter 3
The Monkey Wrench

There are a myriad of ways to hinder good governance. Some of these are specific to organizations, while others are seemingly generic. Each time I think I have "seen it all" in terms of how governance is misconstrued or mis-applied, someone or some organization proves me wrong!

The colloquial expression "throw a monkey wrench into the works" or "throw a spanner into the works" denotes the capacity to mess up life's best laid plans. Those expressions have, over time, generally been used in relation to someone's innate capacity for placing "sand into the wheels of progress" – another idiom that carries with it the connotation of moving a situation away from a preferred course. We likely all know someone who has this capacity and, the moment he or she shows up, the potential of a plan to succeed is in considerable jeopardy.

The number of reasons why elected councils fail in their task of governing effectively is seemingly infinite. Every election can bring a new set of people to the council table. While the turnover rate on local government councils is generally less than 50 percent, the addition of just one new member can disrupt the harmony enjoyed by the council of the foregoing term. New relationships need to be formed; current policies are expected to be challenged; the preferences of the last group of councillors will need to be set aside as the new term begins.

Not only is there considerable expectation of changes in the "face" of council; so, too, will there be struggles. One of the most persistent challenges is the absence of clarity with respect to who has what role – that is, what is the council expected to do, and what roles does the administration play? While this challenge regarding clarity of roles might be readily dismissed by some, it has nonetheless plagued many elected municipal councils over the years, and will likely continue to do so.

Part of the reason for this confusion around roles is the lack of clearheaded material made available to all candidates for office. It is possible for a person to register to be a candidate and not have any idea what the task of being an elected member entails. This is not to suggest that there are no orientation materials available to those running for elected office – there are, and perhaps more so with each passing term of office. Such materials may often be accessed at the municipal office in most communities or online through the municipal affairs office in each province.

So, why run if you do not really understand what a local councillor actually does? Well, for some, the opportunity to make decisions affecting local government or to fight the municipality from within (and be paid for it) proves to be too attractive to pass up. While most candidates make themselves aware of the expectations of the office, there are still quite a few who profess having had little to no idea that there were more than two meetings a month or that there were restrictions on what they could say in public and what issues were legitimate to decide. The fact that there is a process to determining planning matters (and that much of that process is legislated) is also beyond the understanding of many!

I Ran My Business, So ...

There are a number of well-meaning folks who run their own businesses and who become frustrated with the glacial speed of "town hall." As a result, they offer up their services and considerable skills in business to the people of their community, convinced that, if only the folks at the town office ran their "business" the way a local business was run, good decisions would always be made and there would be time left over for coffee. Such a mindset, regardless of how well-intentioned, is sadly misplaced and misled and will, over a fairly short period of time, lead to no end of problems. It is not that the businessperson does not understand how to get things done in the business world. It is the fact that the world of politics and democratic decision making has many more twists and turns that will absolutely thwart and frustrate the quick decision-making style deemed so important to the "edge of the seat" businessperson.

The second and equally problematic challenge facing the businessperson who has yet to figure out why government and business differ is that of "rolling up their sleeves and doing the job." That philosophy would be useful and workable if the job to be done was the one that council was elected to do. However, the job to be done is that of setting policy and approving a course of direction – not paving the road or building the new public works shop.

While that "get at it" mindset is admirable, it will also lead to problems if someone with that kind of motivation thinks that he or she will be expected to serve in a "working" capacity.

What Skills Do I Have?

While there are always exceptions to the rule, the vast majority of folks are elected *in spite of* their day-to-day careers, not because of them. Most electors are not really mindful of what the council candidate does for his or her "regular" (or daytime) work. As a result, we have teachers, pharmacists, hospital employees, marketing experts, former fire chiefs, and farmers on councils across the country (and sometimes on the same council). Citizens are not looking to "hire" their councillor. They would expect to pay more, quite frankly, if that were true.

The skills possessed by each elected official help to inform their choices and their remarks in a debate. Each person looks at an issue somewhat differently because of their life's work and their own interests. As a result of this mixture of perspectives, debates can become quite heated and sometimes (unfortunately) volatile. The issue is seldom one of "who's right," but rather one of determining the core issue and how to best collectively work towards a reasonable solution.

Once elected life is over (and it will be), the now ex-elected official will be looking to resume their career. Regardless of how many committees served on or positions held as a result of being elected to a local council, the organization doing the hiring is still largely interested in "How does your work experience fit with what we are attempting to find?" Having formerly worked for years as an executive recruitment professional, I can advise with confidence that being an elected official says you care about your community and it cared for you. Now ... about that missing six years on your work resumé ...

The person who absolutely believes that their work experience got them elected is to be feared by the administration. Such a person will forever try to find out how he or she can "help" you. No amount of feedback to the contrary will be accepted.

In my own experience, it was not my work as a management consultant that got me elected or kept me in public office. Even though I was advising other communities across Canada, often on matters pertaining to local government, the electors in *my* community were largely disinterested. They wanted to know that I was prepared to lead *this* community. They were more interested that I owned a house in town than the fact that I had a degree.

This Is More Interesting

Having come safely through the waters of an election campaign and tasted the fruits of that labour, newly-elected officials may find the role described in their orientation sounds boring by comparison to what they see the administration doing. As a result, an elected official may declare to staff that, given the obvious need for more help, and based on limited budgeted resources, the council member is only too willing to step into the gap and furnish the assistance necessary. This offer should be quickly and firmly rejected with whatever reasoned argument the staff member can muster. ("Your offer is appreciated, but we need you far more as our elected council member," etc.)

The administration adds to this source of role confusion by spending too much time during an orientation advising council members on the day-to-day duties of a department head! While the department heads and CAO may think they are being helpful to the understanding of council members, what they are really doing is convincing the latter that doing the work of a department head and adding their intelligence and experience to the tasks just described is what is needed and expected. The focus of any orientation must be on what council does and the challenges a council faces, not on the role of a the administration.

I'm as Knowledgeable as You

While it is not often the case, it may be that the person getting elected actually *does* have more academic background as well as more experience than the director of finance (or director of ... or CAO); and thus, stepping in to fill the obvious need is viewed as a natural outcome of being elected. Such a person may think, "The public elected me to do your job." Or, "I used to manage the finances for the air force base, and everyone knows how complex that was. So, managing the finances of the local municipality should be relatively simple by comparison. Slide over!" Or, "The public understands that I have more skills in management/business than anyone else on council or in the office." And, that may be correct. However, regardless of how accurate an assessment that may be, the simple truth of the matter lies in answering a very simple question: What brought you to the office? If you applied and were hired, you are part of the administration and your duties are assigned by the CAO. If you ran for office and were elected, sit right there on the other side of the council table.

The Public Expects Me To!

Of all the reasons typically given by council members who feel they were elected to manage "town hall," this one is the most difficult to counteract. The public understands that they are electing a mayor and council. They believe that the people they elect will make all the decisions that impact their civic lives. If asked who is in charge of the municipality, their answer most frequently will be "the mayor." Those a bit more knowledgeable or experienced may respond that it's "the mayor and council members." Seldom will they identify "the manager" (or CAO). As a result, when someone is elected to office, he or she may expect to be put in charge of programs, agencies, or departments that actually deliver the services.

Hopefully, those running for office will be afforded with first-rate orientation materials, clearly explaining the respective roles of council and management, and why such role separation is not only useful, but also legislated. Further, the orientation provided by the administration should also be focused primarily (and at the outset) on council's role, followed with a brief description of administrative functions and challenges. (Unfortunately, this does not often happen; and thus, administrators contribute to their own role problems, which are soon and predictably to follow.)

Knowing how to respond to concerns, complaints, and questions by the public is critical. An elected official is unwise to simply brush off such queries with "That's not my concern. Talk to one of our staff members at municipal hall!" That kind of response will guarantee a one-term council member. The public elected you. It is you from whom they expect a response. How you respond, however, will determine whether you will perpetuate the myth that you "run" the municipality ... or will gradually educate the public that your role differs from that of management. Your "job description" states that you can and will pass along their complaint to the right department and ask that agency to respond.

Misconceptions relative to roles will plague each and every council at some stage during their term of office. The only antidote to such issues arising or continuing is continually reinforced roles for members of council, the mayor, and the CAO. I would argue that a thorough orientation at the outset of a council term (preferably within one to two weeks of the election) should be supplemented by ongoing training for council members, at a minimum held monthly or prior to the "call to order" for the next six months of council meetings.

Chapter 4
10 Principles of Good Governance for Effective Councils

Policy governance is neither understood well nor applied consistently. This is due, in part, to the fact that *what* a council is to do is legislated (at least in terms of the greater roles); *how* a council goes about these tasks is left largely to the dictates and preferences of each council. Some have been well trained; some inherit good practices and simply improve those; others access enhanced training opportunities or qualified people. Some, unfortunately, perpetuate the problems of the past.

There are approximately 4,000 local governments across Canada. Not all function at the level they should. Those that do function well often do so because of certain attributes in their leadership DNA and particular qualities in their relationships to each other and their community. They also fare well because of adherence to good governance principles (see below), including a focus on the value of policies.

1. A Respect for Its Role and Roles of Others

Effective councils respect role separation. An effective council understands that it takes more than quarterbacks to win a football game. They recognize that it takes more than the world's best goaltender to win a hockey championship. Effective councils clearly understand that, while their role is very significant, the roles played by others are essential to the community's well-being.

Each council has enough challenges on its own plate, without interfering with the responsibilities delegated to the administration or to other bodies. A key question that should be asked at a council meeting (but seldom is heard) is: "Why are we being asked to deal with this issue?" Or, phrased in another way, "What is *our* role in this matter?"

If the answer is unclear, then the matter may not need to be on council's agenda and quite likely should be referred back to the administration. Unfortunately (and frequently), management may place items in front of council that are already covered by policy, but that they felt council would find "interesting." While there may be circumstances in which the CAO has the authority to make a decision, yet feels there is wisdom in council reviewing the merits of the matter, such instances ought to be few and far between. If the issue has already been the subject of a policy review, and the CAO and administration have been directed accordingly by council, then council being asked once again to consider the matter would seem unnecessary (or reflecting the fear by the CAO of "getting it wrong").

Council must resist "upward delegation" by its management. Such a practice does not encourage better administration or role clarity.

Where the decision making of council would benefit from the wisdom of others, and where time permits, referral to an appropriate advisory body can often yield sage insights not previously "on the table." Thus, the input of a committee of council might be useful and timely.

2. Willingness to Work Collegially with Others

An effective council understands the value in working collegially with other bodies that have a legitimate interest in the issue and a role to play. While council is generally recognized by most as the principal player in any local issue, it may not be the only one with an interest or a stake. Other organizations in the community certainly have key roles to play and could be instrumental in helping council achieve its objectives (e.g., tourism society, museum board, library board, hospital/regional health board, etc.). Further, many communities live in close proximity to their neighbours and could benefit from a regional approach to a number of issues, such as economic development, recreation, tourism, social services, policing, water treatment, and garbage disposal. Good relationships do not come by chance. They develop over time and as a result of frank discussion and a willingness to assist and be of service.

A council that fails to take advantage of an offer to collaborate with its neighbours may be missing a significant opportunity to leverage a small project into a much larger and more diverse one, or may be foregoing a significant financial contribution by other partners. Inter-municipal agreements are not only useful in spreading the costs of major projects onto a larger tax and population base; they can also set the groundwork for agreements on a myriad of other services. In some instances, such agreements may help to sustain the life of a smaller municipality; in other cases, a large rural community may be quite willing to support a smaller urban neighbour, entering into a legitimate process of negotiating "who does what" – and to whose benefit.

3. Development of a Solid Team with Administration

Similar to the foregoing point, an effective and wise council finds ways to build a solid working relationship with its administration. This can not be achieved if the council's attitude at the outset is one of "you work for us; you'll do as we say." While this is an all too accurate description in many communities, those who are seemingly more "enlightened" recognize that a respectful, professional approach works much better than a master-slave relationship.

Again, a constructive relationship does not result from an election. It comes out of the work of both parties intent on developing a respectful relationship, based on an appreciation of the distinct roles that each is expected to play.

One of the key ways that a council can achieve this is to ensure that it has an excellent and open relationship with its CAO, founded on mutual trust and respect. This necessitates an ongoing (and at least annual) process of evaluation and feedback in a candid fashion, designed to ensure that the CAO continues to grow as a professional and that the relationship continues to mature.

4. Creating a Community-Based Strategic Agenda

Effective councils ensure that their policy framework supports proactive and comprehensive community engagement. Community engagement occurs when the public is invited to become involved in identifying key issues and helping to establish priorities for change or improvement. It also occurs when council is interested in pursuing a new or revised policy thrust and is anxious to have public input to determine whether or not such an approach is consistent with the will of the community.

Where a community-based strategic agenda is the preferred end result, council, with input from the administration, needs to identify who its stakeholders are and how best to involve them in a strategic process. Such a process will examine locally-driven (and therefore "owned") ways of establishing core vision, values, goals, and priorities.

A policy framework that begins with "we consult regularly and widely with ..." is instrumental in inviting the community to help establish a sound and "made in this municipality" vision, as well as key priorities.

5. Desire to Build Communication Channels

Effective communities communicate regularly and in a manner that addresses the issues of concern to residents. Local media is not relied upon to do a job that rightfully belongs to the municipality. Some establish a formalized process of communicating messages through the municipal website, social media tools, or through the local media by issuing "The Mayor's Report" or "Views of Council." Others provide an update on council's plans using inserts included with utility bills or tax notices. The key, as reflected in the pithy wisdom quoted below, is to keep such messages succinct.

> "Every man has a right to be heard, but no man has the right to strangle democracy with a single set of vocal chords." – Adlai Stevenson, former U.S. diplomat

Effective municipalities ensure that their own techniques of communicating messages out to the public are used in a consistent, ethical, and transparent way. Such municipalities create and adhere to a policy of ongoing communication on the key issues through messages that are appropriate – and accurate. Council is wise to **not** put out such messages close to an election (along with the smiling faces of all its members) if that is the first time such an initiative has been instituted. Council should also ensure that messages are timely, particularly with regard to major new initiatives.

6. Sharing Updates on Municipal Performance

If council has embarked on a comprehensive program of business planning or has created specific targets within its strategic plan, the public should be advised as to what progress has been made against those targets. This should occur on a regularly scheduled basis. Frequent and informative updates should be shared on the local website and/or other communication forum, as best suited to the objective. Such messaging should parallel the mayor's "state of the municipality" address, speaking to the progress on key council priorities.

Once those priorities are established, the onus should be on the administration to identify the milestones of progress and to design mechanisms that will enable useful and insightful reporting. Effective local governments encourage two-way interactive communication: the public is able to get their messages in, and council transmits its messages out.

7. Being Open to Change

An effective council is one that is in a constant state of learning. It aspires to improve upon the past and build a base for future changes. It recognizes that both urban and rural environments are not static, but are continually experiencing environmental changes. Without foregoing its core principles, an effective council examines its practices with an open mind and seeks to find new ways to do its business. (Such a perspective drives this book on policy governance; how can a council govern wisely in such a fast-changing world?)

This is not to say that an effective council is only about change. Rather, it is about being open to change. Thus, such a council may see that current approaches work in this term and are sufficiently flexible for the public to understand and intervene. Its approach to policy development or strategic planning may be deemed workable. Its approach to council meetings or to hearing delegations may be considered leading edge, and thus not in need of repair. But, an effective council realizes that such accomplishments are often short-lived; and thus, it monitors what is happening elsewhere. This desire to stay flexible and to challenge old or current ways of doing business is one of the key elements of a successful council, as compared to one that has grown old where it stands.

8. Balanced Approach to Citizen Participation

An effective council understands that it will stay in office as long as it successfully engages and interprets the public will. This is not a simple process, nor do most councils appear to get it right. In fact, many councils struggle with understanding the term "public" and may be led into presuming that it describes:

- the person I last spoke with on the phone who was really upset by a recent decision of council;
- the members of my social group or favourite club; or
- the people who are in attendance at a meeting of council to show support for a particular presentation.

None of the above accurately describes "the public." From a council perspective, the public constitutes those folks who live in our community and who rely on this council to make wise choices and decisions. Many of these people will never be heard from or perhaps even be seen in the course of a council term, other than at the door while a candidate is out campaigning. To have effective policy governance that embraces citizen input, council must challenge itself: How will we ensure that we have checked in with the public from time to time? On what key issues do we absolutely expect their input?

The search for public opinion should not simply be focused around this issue or that. It will be far more useful (and likely representative) if public opinion is sought on a regularly-scheduled basis, and on a wide variety of issues and public priorities.

It is very unfortunate if council mistakenly believes that the will of the public is reflected or represented by the five or six souls sitting in the gallery during an appearance by a delegation.

9. Willingness to Accept Democracy

An effective council understands that it is in office because the public placed it there, and that it will remain in office as long as the public has confidence that it is doing just what it said it would. Accepting democracy means that I accept who, besides me, the public has elected for this term of office. Accepting democracy means I can be disappointed that one of my former colleagues was not elected and that someone new has been, and yet be magnanimous enough to welcome in the new person.

It is a sad commentary to note that those involved in this level of democracy are sometimes amongst those who least respect its principles. All too frequently, a council is troubled by the presence of one or more of its own members who refuse to respect the right of others to be wrong, and to accept that those who they feel are wrong may indeed win the vote on this or that important matter. If a council is to function as it should, there must be an acceptance that one's colleagues may well reflect very differing views at times, but they are still trying to achieve what they see as the best interests of the municipality.

Further, both the council as a whole and the mayor in particular must recognize that not everyone needs to be in total agreement in order for the municipality to move its agenda forward. Democracy does not equate with unanimity.

10. Desire to Serve

Public life is a matter of the heart. It is a reflection of one's desire to serve others and the sense that "If not me, then who?" Effective council members must have a desire to serve others and a willingness to devote their hours and energies to this noble cause. With this desire comes the recognition (often sooner than later) that not everyone is going to be impressed by your efforts and those of your colleagues. Some will take considerable umbrage with your position on this issue or that one. Some may be discourteous to you in the council chambers and may be overheard badmouthing you and your views to others. Service always draws critics. There will always be those who disagree with your approach to the issues or your sense of the priorities.

While negativity tends to have a wearing effect, experienced council members recognize that the ballot box is the ideal place to determine if their services are generally and genuinely appreciated by a majority.

When the time does come, however, if the thought of running again for office seems somehow distasteful or onerous, the "red light" should shine and the retirement speech written. Being talked into the next race by a few enterprising souls who would rather you do the sacrificing than they is not the basis upon which such a decision should be made. In order to keep a positive focus on what lies ahead, a certain degree of enthusiasm is necessary – not just for the prospect of being re-elected, but also for the thought that the term can be long and the rewards few.

Chapter 5

Impact of the Chosen Governance Model

The focus of this chapter is on the salient question: **What makes the difference in determining whether or not council truly adds value?** While one could argue that a council comprised of those with a common commitment to serve is the key factor, my experience would suggest otherwise. Every council I have encountered in a lengthy career has been blessed by those who express their desire to serve (the actions and rhetoric of some notwithstanding). That has not, however, stopped such a council from being so focused on what their administration is doing that the degree of value being added is scant in comparison to their best intentions.

Others might suggest that electing those who have the same perspective on the key issues is the critical factor. Again, while having everyone on the same page may be argued as constituting an asset, one could also argue that diverse views can lead to better solutions in the longer term. Based on experience, they, too, would often be right.

One could also offer an argument in favour of experience, suggesting that a council of experience is more likely to be of added value as compared to one populated by political neophytes. Again, however, I have met councils comprised of a majority who are long in the tooth, with a driving motivation and agenda that appears to be one of survival, thereby leading to a largely innocuous, do-nothing style.

It is my premise or thesis that any council truly interested in making a lasting difference will have a dynamic policy agenda and a refined policy framework. "Busyness" does not count; attending innumerable meetings matters little; holding positions locally, provincially, and federally may seem important at the time, but they, too, will be short-lived. What matters is how each council treats the matters of governance that appear before it at every meeting of council, and whether it carried out its duties in a consistent, thoughtful, compassionate manner.

Garbage In, Garbage Out

After a lifetime of working directly with municipal councils, I am struck by the impact of "the governance model" on a council's ability to lead. There is an old and somewhat worn adage that suggests "garbage in, garbage out." I have always considered this expression to be an admonition not to disregard the importance of the process of decision making if you want to ensure that the ultimate decisions are thoughtful and truly effective. Thus, I have come to believe that, where key elements in a decision process are ignored, the final decision may be greatly flawed. Or, at the very least, good decisions will be far more likely as the product of a process that considers all the basic salient points of view and available factual information.

I have squirmed in the audience of governing bodies that make snap decisions on information that they have first had access to just minutes before. I have watched (likely with widening eyes) as governing bodies heard a delegation on an important matter and acted on a perceived obligation of an "action-oriented" council to make a quick decision while the group is still present. I have sat through council meetings where there has been more focus on a provision in the procedural by-law that limits any member of council to one question per delegation, than on the objective of ensuring that all of the important questions have been answered. I have been dismayed by a council's acceptance of locally-made rules of order that negate the importance of making quality decisions with confidence – rather than poor decisions that meet the provisions of a hastily drafted (and, in my opinion, inappropriate) procedural by-law.

Which Model to Use?

The issue of which "governance model" to use is one that challenges every council. While many council members may be unaware, the choices available are quite numerous. History underscores the evidence of a wide variety of models being used, to both the benefit and seemingly the disadvantage of their host communities. Perhaps ironically, the model of governance that appears to work best for one council may not "fit" the needs or character of the next. This serves to underline the importance of each council reviewing the impact of the model and determining which one works best for it.

Some of the factors that appear to determine the governance model and, therefore, the governing style of council include the following.

History

Likely the most significant factor determining what style or model of governance a new council will adopt is the model that was in place when the current council assumed office. This is due to two principal factors.

First, in the absence of any real issue around this topic, the administration's briefing will be based on the model of the outgoing council. So, unless the type of governance model has become an election issue (which would be highly unusual), the administration is most likely to base any orientation process around the model as it currently stands (i.e., that practiced by the most immediate council).

In addition, some of the members of this council may also have been members of the previous council. Regardless of whether the returning members struggled due in part to the existing model of governance, and unless they make that an issue, they will be confronted by the model under which they previously operated.

Degree of acceptance of that particular model over time

Over time, both the council and administration become familiar with the nuances of a particular model and find ways to make it work. Committees that may no longer report regularly to all of council are still tolerated. Committee chairs who begin to see themselves as the heads of departments reign unchallenged and become the power blocs on council. Agencies, boards, and committees that no longer function as intended are allowed to continue in existence because changing the status quo might cause the few remaining members to object loudly to the media.

Sometimes, the model just "works." Other than a bit of refinement from time to time, the municipality continues to function much as it always has and everyone involved settles into a pattern of acceptance and familiarity.

Degree of turnover of members of council in most recent election

Significant turnovers of council members often provide the most fertile ground for considering a new approach. Where there are few returning members, there may be greater appetite to consider change, since the belief that "everything we did worked just fine" does not seem supported by the results. Most would likely admit that the public wanted some change or they would not have voted out so many of their colleagues. Typically, few changes in the make-up of council equates with little change in how council discharges what it perceives as its role.

The foregoing will not stop the administration from briefing council as though all were happy with the existing model. The governance model is something that the administration may consider as sacrosanct (and, given the other issues confronting the municipality, how council makes decisions is not a hill to die upon).

Public comment on separation of council from the public

Sometimes, the governance model comes between council and its public. Or, at least, that is how it is perceived by the public. Over time, council may develop processes in terms of how it makes unpopular decisions – ones that are not well received by the public and may lead to considerable criticism in the media and on the street – to which a new council will need to respond or risk a similar fate. For example, in the case of the City of Edmonton years ago when they employed a commission-board model, the media and public began to believe that senior management made virtually all decisions of any note. The new mayor was determined to establish a much stronger role for his council, and thus campaigned successfully to have the old system abolished. The City of Winnipeg did something similar a decade or so later when it abolished its commission-board model.

The public wants to feel that its elected representatives are accessible and are in charge. While they may not understand all of the intricacies of how council makes its decisions, they do understand results, and they do listen to (and read) the negative publicity. If there is enough commentary in the media about how council is misusing its authority, or if there is any sense that the CAO is running council, the public will find ways to express their unease.

Public style of mayor as chief elected official

This can work in favour of a new model, as well as against it. If the model appears to give a very strong mayor too much power, while limiting any of the normal checks and balances imposed by an alert council, the demand may be made to adjust the power fulcrum. If, on the other hand, the mayor's position is viewed as overly dependent on the rest of council in order to "work," then the public may be in the mood to encourage changes.

This has as much to do with personal style as it does models of governance. A very strong-willed mayor will not likely tolerate a system that may be inhibiting his or her capacity to lead. While each may take a different approach to how their displeasure is expressed, there is little question that it will be made evident.

Relationship between mayor and CAO

There are a number of reasons why the relationship between the mayor and the CAO is vital to the well-being of the municipality. (This topic can be reviewed in *Cuff's Guide for Municipal Leaders – Volumes 1 and 2*.) One of these relates to the degree of confidence that the community feels in its leaders and their ability to work together for the good of the residents. If, as is the case in most municipalities, the two leaders of the political and administrative realms are viewed as working hand-in-hand in terms of trying to resolve community priorities and issues, then the majority of residents will be unlikely to examine the governance model much more closely (unless individual councillors are raising the issue).

Where the relationship is strained, all aspects affecting governance will be on the table. In some cases, mayors simply do an "end around" on the CAO, approaching individual department heads directly, rather than affording the CAO the courtesy due his or her position.

Why the Choice of Model Matters

The question might arise: "Why is the governance model (or, in other words, the way by which we do business in council) so important?" The simple response is: because the model of governance either facilitates or impedes how council does its business.

Some councils have struggled with their style of governing, while others have seemingly been able to move forward with much greater ease and results. While the personalities elected for each term may have an impact, the type of community, number of big issues with which it is confronted, and the mechanisms that a council uses to make its decisions also have a significant impact.

Governance models also tend to be a reflection of the style of the council. That is, those councils that are not particularly interested in what the public has to say other than at election time will more likely tend to either ignore the input of community groups or refuse any attempt to establish a broader consultative process. Further, those councils that have historically relied on a wide array of standing committees may simply continue their existence without considering whether or not they add value to council's decision making.

The impact of your governance model is significant. Your model determines:

- how well council understands the issues;
- how much time you set aside to debate the big issues;
- whether or not you split up council into smaller groups to get a deeper understanding of departmental issues;
- how much you rely on the public for added input; and

> whether or not you expect to discuss the broad policy issues or the day-to-day running of the system.

A sound governance model should ensure that the *priorities of council* are kept in the forefront. Council is expected to lead. This does not mean that council's role is simply one of baptizing the views and reports of the administration. Rather, the public anticipates that its leaders will have some of their own ideas on what constitutes the most significant needs of the community. Thus, an annual session with council is essential, with the only issue on the agenda being the identification of council's key priorities. The initial session should occur within 60 days of an election, followed by a re-visiting of these priorities on a regular (i.e., bi-monthly) basis thereafter. Further, at least annually, the strategic priorities of council ought to be revisited.

The point here is that the model should support this process. At the top of council's agenda should be the need to assess its progress on the bigger challenges facing the municipality. It should not take a resolution of council to initiate such a review. This process needs to be intentional and virtually automatic. How can that be done? What is the policy of council?

Impacts on the Style of Governance

The chosen model can also have a definite if not profound impact on the style of governance of any council and its administration. These impacts include the following.

Degree of ownership of decisions by council

It has been my experience that a council feels committed to decisions in which it has been intimately involved in developing. That is, the extent to which council is involved will often reflect the level of its commitment to the outcomes. Council's involvement also determines the degree of ownership of corporate and council decisions. If the decisions are largely that of the administration, and council has simply approved a report with minimal debate, there is less likelihood of council feeling really committed to the action than in a situation whereby council has reviewed the background report, had a series of discussions, perhaps discussed the matter in a standing committee, and has responded to the queries of the public regarding the issue.

If the governance model emphasizes efficiency over depth of understanding, then decisions may be made promptly – but, they may be repeated because they were not fully understood. A sound governance model will be one that affords council the time to reflect *before* deciding – not in the parking lot after the fact!

Sense of proximity to public as perceived by council

A governance model also impacts whether or not council members feel that they are adequately connected to members of the public. Any model that places a higher priority on efficiency of governance than the connectedness of council with its public reflects faulty thinking. Sometimes, council can be unwittingly, yet inappropriately led into this situation by an administration who is simply trying to get the job done (i.e., the delivery of services based on council's policies and priorities). Council members, however, are in their positions as a result of their ability to connect with fellow residents. They are not expected to become experts in public governance or in efficiency measures. They must, however, be able to find those mechanisms that allow councillors ongoing interaction with the public.

Sense of proximity to public as perceived by public

As a corollary to the foregoing point, the public also needs to sense that it is front and centre in any discussion regarding council's decision-making system. That is, the potential impact of council's style of governance depends on whether or not the public believes it is being shut out of the process, or that its views are not considered or embraced by council. The decision to eliminate a committee or board needs to consider a number of factors, including the public's perception of whether or not of its importance and impact are unduly interfered with or negated in making a change to a new model.

Sense of proximity to administration as perceived by council

The choice of a governance model can also impact how council views its leadership to and direction of the administration. That is, the choice of governance model will play a significant role in determining whether council members perceive that they are suitably in touch with the senior administration, or if the model discourages such contact. Because most models direct that the only suitable contact with the administration is via the office of the CAO, members of council may feel estranged from department heads and other key members of the staff.

While ensuring that directions to the administration are to proceed through the office of the CAO (for purposes of accountability and out of respect for the by-law and CAO's jurisdiction), most models permit or encourage ongoing linkages on other (often non-policy) matters with the other members of the senior administration (at the department head level).

Powers exerted by the mayor's office

As one of its central tenets, our system of local government includes what is commonly referred to as "a weak mayor" system. While this bears no relationship to the person holding the office, as by nature he or she may be deemed to be very strong-willed, it underlines the notion that the mayor is elected as "one of" the council, and not apart from it.

Whereas the legislation refers to the unique nature of the mayor and may indicate his or her responsibility to chair meetings, in most instances the mayor is accorded very few additional powers. Some provinces indicate little else in terms of powers, while others may provide for the mayor to establish committees of council and choose the committee chairs; others provide for the mayor to suspend municipal officers for unbecoming conduct (which can be appealed to the rest of council), and so on. The by-law establishing the model may, at the consent of council, defer other powers to the mayor (e.g., chairing an agendas committee). The model of governance will impact how those powers are used. That is, the model may impact whether or not the mayor's office and use of power is perceived as weak or overly dictatorial.

Flow of decision making across the organization

As a final note in this section pertaining to the impact of the model, how governance is understood and established in any community may also impact how decisions of council are communicated across the system. For example, if council has established a standing committee system of governance and has granted committees considerable authority to guide the decisions of council and the administration, there may well be instances wherein decisions are being made *by* committees, and being implemented as the rest of council is hearing about the decision. Or, a very strong council-CAO system may have empowered the CAO to make most, if not all, the day-to-day administrative decisions. This might be done without prior referral to council, on the understanding that the CAO by-law accords the CAO those powers. In such an instance, the council's policy framework will need to be suitably broad so as to provide the direction needed and the assurance that the CAO is acting within the constraints of council's previously established decisions.

While some may argue that good people can make a poor model work, whereas people of ill intent can cause a good model to fail (and I agree), the *choice of model* is important. The choice of model can have a definite if not profound impact on the style of governance of any council and its administration.

Chapter 6
Common Governance Models

While those interested in pursuing an examination of governance/administrative models would be advised to consider other texts related to this topic, what follows is a cursory overview of the various models at work today in local governments across Canada. While there will likely be some degree of variation in how one community implements its model versus that of another, the basics are largely as described below.

Council Manager (Chief Administrative Officer) Model

This popular model, which is used virtually across Canada in some form or another, is built upon the council-manager model begun in the United States in the early 1900s. The Canadian version reflects the view that councils are elected to set the vision and policies for the community, whereas the manager (or CAO) is expected to function in support of the vision, policies, and budgets. The CAO is the appointed head of the administration, having preferably been chosen based on his or her training and related education, often (but not only) in the field of public administration. The CAO is not only the council's chief advisor; he or she is also the point person with respect to getting things done.

The CAO's principal functions are as follows:

- provide recommendations to council on all of its business issues;
- ensure that the reports of department heads are of a high quality (i.e., complete, fair, well-crafted);

- recommend the budget and service levels;
- implement the approved budget;
- hire/fire all staff (a feature of the U.S. model more so than the Canadian model);
- coordinate the work of all departments (and related agencies); and
- provide performance feedback to all department heads.

The relevant provincial legislation often sets out the limits on the authority of the CAO to hire or fire subordinate employees. Alternatively, this matter may be dealt with by by-law or contract. Quite frequently, municipalities rely on a contractual arrangement, spelling out the duties and limits of power with clarity, along with the usual provisions relating to term, termination, reviews, etc.

Each model has advantages and disadvantages. The intent here is to outline these in a straightforward, balanced manner.

Advantages

The principal advantages of the council-manager model are generally found to be:

- the vesting of administrative leadership in one individual who is held accountable for discharging the associated responsibilities (as outlined in the act or by by-law);
- the separation of council from detailed involvement in administrative matters (in which they may have little expertise or training);
- closer contact between council and department heads, thus allowing for a better grasp of the whole organization by council;
- leaving "politics" largely in the hands of politicians, with council's stature therefore enhanced;
- a system that is more responsive and open to the council than is the case with other models;
- the sense that council is free to focus on the key policy issues, rather than being lost in the interesting, yet perhaps mundane, aspects of civic administration;

- the fact that a manager is not subject to recall every three years, and thus should be able to take a longer range view of the issues; and
- the streamlined, efficient character of the system (i.e., there is no other buffer or blockage between council and the departments).

Disadvantages

The principal disadvantages of the council-manager model include:

- the vesting of considerable responsibility (and therefore power) in one individual whose authority might be seen to exceed that of council;
- the potential of one person to act as the gatekeeper of all information flow to council, thereby limiting council's access to more than one source of information;
- the complexity of the system, making it difficult to expect one person to have a sufficiently broad and in-depth knowledge of so many subjects;
- the academic training of the individual may bias that individual in terms of other disciplines;
- much of the success of the organization is, in effect, reliant on having chosen the right person; and
- policy recommendations flowing to council may lack political input (particularly if there are no standing committees).

On balance, the council-manager model is deemed by most observers of local government to be that which is most appropriate to dispensing with the business of governing and managing municipal policies and services.

Council-Executive Committee

The council-executive committee model is generally found in only a few of the larger cities. This model reflects a committee of council comprised of the mayor and some of his or her colleagues, generally less than a quorum. Often, the executive committee consists of the mayor, deputy mayor, and the chairs of council's standing committees – thus, those who are viewed as the power-brokers on council. They may be appointed by council, but are, more frequently, appointed by the mayor.

The principal argument in favour of this model is the belief that a smaller body than the full council in a larger municipality can act more expediently on behalf of the whole council, without giving up any of the "real" authority of council. Comprised of some of the key players on a council, the executive committee wields considerable clout and is viewed by outsiders as akin to the cabinet style of governance practised by both the provincial and federal levels of government.

The executive committee may be granted, by by-law, the authority to:

- make decisions within council's overall budget, such as the awarding of significant tenders;
- review and recommend the budget to council for its consideration and adoption;
- review and recommend policy issues to council for its consideration and adoption;
- enter into contracts on matters approved by the budget;
- liaise with, guide, or direct the CAO;
- approve changes to the structure of the organization as a whole, or to individual departments;
- execute agreements with other bodies, agencies, or contractors;
- approve for appointment or dismissal or recommend the appointment or dismissal of the CAO, solicitor, clerk, and perhaps department heads;
- enter into collective bargaining agreements with municipal employees; and
- perform other duties as assigned to it by council.

Perhaps the closest parallel to this model was the "board of control" model, which featured a commission-style structure (i.e., three or four senior managers appointed as essentially equals to manage the

Chapter 6 • Common Governance Models

affairs of the municipality), but where the members were elected to the board.

Advantages

The principal advantages of this council-executive committee model are:

- places accountability for decision making in fewer hands, thereby making accountability easier to discern;
- focuses key decision-making processes at the political level, providing a mechanism to initiate and encourage the adoption of policies;
- ensures the mayor of some support for his or her initiatives (depending on whether or not the committee is comprised of the mayor's nominees and whether or not the mayor has any power to revoke their appointment);
- tends to take on some of the responsibilities and powers normally ascribed to a standing committee system and may provide a clearer focus to these areas; and
- increases the likelihood that the policy positions articulated by the mayor during an election campaign will gain the support of council.

Disadvantages

The principal disadvantages of the council-executive committee model are:

- increased power of executive committee members creates a sense of two classes of councillors (those in the loop, and those not);
- councillors not on the executive committee may feel marginalized to the point of disrupting the executive committee initiatives;
- ultimate roles and powers of council may be viewed as diminished due to certain of its powers having been delegated to the executive committee;

- reporting relationships of senior management may be diffused and possibly confused (i.e., does senior management report to council, the executive committee, a standing committee, etc.?);
- decisions may be made by executive committee and be publicly known before the rest of council is advised; and
- information to all of council may be filtered by the executive committee, and thus the rest of council may not be given sufficient access to information, so as to have a full and concurrent understanding.

Council-Standing Committee-CAO

Many councils have relied quite extensively upon either a series of standing committees or a committee of the whole (all members of council in attendance – see next model discussed below). Where council creates standing committees, these are most often limited to the number of departments reporting to the CAO or to a lesser number.

In each instance, the CAO is expected to play a significant role as policy advisor and as the titular head of the administration. The CAO determines who will attend the meetings of each committee.

In some instances, the powers of the committee system have expanded at the expense of the CAO. In some communities, these committees function as though they held the authority of the CAO, and thus direct senior management without referral to the CAO. While the CAO reports directly to the mayor and council, the mayor acts as the intermediary in day-to-day guidance.

Each policy committee is governed by terms of reference that outline their spheres of responsibility. The CAO designates which senior staff members are to advise which standing committees. Agenda materials for standing committees are, in most instances, circulated through the CAO's office prior to their consideration by the relevant standing committee or by the committee of the whole. Councillors often prefer this model, as they favour the notion that this model affords them the best opportunity of illustrating and adding the value of their respective administrative or professional backgrounds.

All of these committees exist only insofar as the council allows them to. That is, they draw their power from council and are expected to have their actions approved by council.

Advantages

The principal advantages of the council-standing committee-CAO model are:

- administrative authority is vested in one individual who is held accountable for discharging council policies and resolutions;
- separation of council from detailed involvement in administrative matters, while affording council the opportunity to review the key issues facing departments, as well as the municipality as a whole;
- provides for a streamlined administrative system, while ensuring adequate political involvement through the committee system;
- politics are left largely in the hands of politicians, so council's stature is enhanced;
- all members of council are equally involved in committee activity and all are concurrently involved as to the issues; and
- key cross-departmental issues can be handled by a committee of the whole, with all members having equal access to confidential issues.

Disadvantages

The principal disadvantages of the council-standing committee-CAO model are:

- considerable authority vested in one individual who may be seen to exceed the power of council;
- potentially, one person can still act as the gatekeeper of all information flowing to council, thereby limiting council's access to more than one source of information;
- considerable difficulty in orchestrating any political agenda, due to the need to always find a majority of votes at the council table;

- reduced control over the CAO and administration, due to the lack of focused power at the political level;
- mayor unable to reflect any more status on his or her issues than others, due to few levers of power attributed to that office;
- potentially diffuses the reporting relationships and responsibilities of the CAO and department heads; and
- individual committees may control key aspects of council's "agenda" and may limit the flow of information to others on council.

The number of standing committees also varies by community and often by council term. Thus, a community may have few committees (two or three) or many (five to eight), again, depending on how they view their role and importance in the decision-making process. The advantages of *few* standing committees are:

- less likelihood of council members becoming directly involved in the management of civic departments;
- greater possibility that committees will focus on broader policy issues;
- improved opportunities for corporate integration of issues; and
- fewer meetings to attend, leaving councillors more time to spend dealing with constituent issues.

The advantages of *more* standing committees are:

- improved awareness by councillors as to the full range (and depth) of issues;
- increased time available to explore issues in depth;
- increased opportunity to review departmental staff in action as they present reports; and
- more opportunities for councillors to act as chair of committees, and thus greater sense of involvement in council's work.

Council-Committee of the Whole-CAO

This model of council's legislative involvement limits council standing committees to one – a committee of the whole. All members of council are the invited participants, with the CAO (or man-

Chapter 6 • Common Governance Models   53

agement team) acting in an advisory capacity. Either the mayor or a member of council chairs this decision-making step (or process). (There are arguments on either side of this question: Does the delegation of this role to someone other than the mayor weaken the role of the mayor, or does it simply provide for other members of council to gain some experience in the role in the event that the mayor's chair is vacated for whatever reason and for however long? Others have argued that having someone else chair allows the mayor to take a more active role in the discussion.)

The committee of the whole may be used exclusively of standing committees (wherein all key policy matters flow through the committee of the whole) or in conjunction with standing committees (wherein the broader, cross-functional issues – such as budget development, personnel, and legal issues – are deferred to the committee of the whole).

For most committee of the whole models, agenda items are largely those submitted by the administration, and requiring council's policy review and approval. Based on the breadth of the organization, these issues will likely be "higher order" issues as time would not permit a review of lesser matters. Council members and external boards/agencies may also have items placed on the agenda by the concurrence of council or through a screening process by an "agenda committee" (e.g., three members of council, with the CAO and clerk acting as advisors).

Committee of the whole meetings generally have both a public and private component. Issues in the latter category would largely be restricted to those pertaining to legal matters, confidential land purchases and sales, and personnel issues. In most jurisdictions, these are the only matters deemed by legislation to warrant a council going *in camera* and withholding the discussion from public view.

Advantages

The advantages of a committee of the whole model are:

➤   council's focus is geared toward policy issues;

- the administrative analysis and advice can readily be orchestrated through the CAO's office;
- all of council can participate in the policy debates;
- all of council is concurrently informed and involved; no one member or group of members has more access to power or information than another; and
- policy issues may be surfaced at this step, thus providing for a time of reflection prior to formal consideration at council.

Disadvantages

The perceived disadvantages of such a model are:

- these meetings (in some communities) tend to be a dress rehearsal for council meetings, so that the importance of a council meeting is diminished; committee of the whole decisions are simply ratified and/or re-discussed;
- focus is necessarily on important and broad issues, thereby deterring councillors from becoming aware of or involved in lesser issues;
- agenda may be so controlled by administration that the definition of "important" versus "lesser" is largely made by the CAO; the fear is that certain items key to council may be buried by the administration and never reach the council table;
- opportunities to view the performance of department heads are few and far between; succession planning is thereby inhibited; and the more obvious temporary or permanent replacements for the CAO may remain largely anonymous; and
- opportunities for public involvement in close proximity to a policy-setting forum are limited.

Cautionary note – I note that "committee of the whole" (sometimes referred to as COW) is *NOT* the same as council *"in camera."* The former simply refers to a council (as a full body) meeting as a committee. The latter refers to a decision by council to meet in private, presumably to discuss those matters intended to be held in confidence by council and as stipulated by the legislation.

Other Governance/Administrative Models

The foregoing is certainly not intended as a complete listing of available governance and administrative models. It is, however, a list of those most common to the Canadian landscape. What occurs, of course, is the choice that each community makes within the constraints of their legal parameters (as set by a local charter and/or provincial legislation). Such choices are, generally speaking, a variation of the foregoing.

Thus, one municipality may delegate additional powers to the mayor or executive committee; others rely more on task forces and external advisory bodies than they do on the standing committees of council. Some use more of a "portfolio" approach, wherein certain councillors are assigned as the chair of a particular function that parallels a civic department (e.g., parks and recreation). In such an instance, any matter going before council that pertains to that portfolio will be considered first by the councillor assigned and then will be recommended forward by that individual. Such a system inevitably confuses policy and administrative roles to the point that the councillor *de facto* becomes the "super department head."

Impact of Size and Type

This rather imprecise manner of categorizing current decision-making models is further constricted or complicated by the multiplicity of municipal sizes and types. That is, there are:

- large urban centres;
- small to mid-size urban centres;
- large rural centres;
- small to mid-size rural centres;
- regional municipalities; and
- a multitude of municipal-directed governing and advisory agencies.

There are significant differences in the foregoing. Some cities are larger than some of our provincial governments. Some rural areas are vast and cumbersome to govern, yet are populated by very few people. Some of the larger urban centres have greater departmental budgets than the entire combined municipal budget of their neighbours.

All, however, are in the business of directing the affairs of citizens, and all tend to operate under quite similar legislation. Governance and the choices it affords are significant matters that require the full attention of any council.

Chapter 7

Case for a New Model: Executive Policy Governance

Our current system of local government does not work. While I might agree that some municipalities make their system work better than others (or better than the last council), in the main, they are not particularly good models. The focus is a mixture of tradition (this is the way we have always done business here) and legislation (the CAO must be responsible for preserving the council minutes; the clerk can only be fired by the council). It does not address the issue of governance from the perspective of "Is this the best way?"

When I say "it does not work," I speak to our currently very narrow manner of funding local government through the tax base and recognize that this is (and will be) deficient. Others far more qualified than I have and will suggest their solutions to the economic woes of local government. However, given that so much of our provincial economies relies on the ability of municipalities to provide quality services, it simply seems logical to ensure that municipal leaders have access to greater funding sources with enhanced balance across rural and urban Canada.

I would also argue that, legislatively, various provinces have handicapped the system of local government both by dictating what services a community is to provide (without the requisite resources), and by ignoring the important role to be played by the CAO (frequently described as council's chief policy advisor and head of the administration). It is amazing that some provinces could approve legislation that requires with certainty the appointment of a clerk and treasurer by the council, and yet state in the same legislation that council "may" appoint a CAO. What nonsense! This simply opens the door to permit a council to view its mayor (an elected official) to also act as the CAO, or to permit a committee of department heads to fulfill this critical role. Neither solution works.

We have also missed the mark legislatively by not providing council with suitable powers to clearly censure and, if necessary, remove a councillor who refuses to abide by democratically-instituted provisions (e.g., respect for confidentiality and for other elected and appointed officials). Leaving each council to the mercy of those who would intentionally disrupt the normal functioning of a community's elected officials or deliberately poison the waters such that well-meaning people will not subject themselves and their families to the abuse is neither well reasoned nor helpful to democracy.

We will not have a truly workable local government system until we clarify and correct such matters. These matters (i.e., limited funding resources, poor or inadequate role definition, and limited powers of censure) must be addressed if local governments are going to legitimately occupy a place of respect as an "order of government."

Finding a Better Way

Municipalities are responsible for their own choices in terms of governance model. While the legislation may provide the parameters within which council is to function, much of what a council does and how it is done is up to local elected officials to determine. In some ways, it is both sad and unnecessary that councils struggle to make sense of their roles and to find ways by which they can add value to the communities they serve. Much of this quandary is self-inflicted, due to an unwillingness and lack of a conscious, thoughtful effort to find a better way within the constraints of the present legislation.

Many a council would deem it to be a waste of taxpayers' resources to explore how they can serve the public more effectively. Some would blindly postulate, "We were elected to keep taxes down, weren't we?" (If that were the case, why not pass a motion to forego any honoraria and meeting per diems as a start ... if that is all the public truly expects. After all, if the council cannot be relied upon to act in a thoughtful, compassionate, and fiscally prudent manner, why elect it?)

When administrators complain of councils becoming too involved in their bailiwick, they often need to look no further than themselves in finding the answer to their own complaint. Many administrations run blindly forward into the next term of office without any thought given to "How can our council do governance better?" If the last council struggled to find their way, with council and administration often at loggerheads in terms of who has what power to do what, then a modicum of wisdom would surely speak to the need to look for different alternatives to the present model.

For example, any model that places the council and administration as adversaries, rather than complementary members of the same team, is not one worthy of consideration or continuation. Unfortunately, some municipalities have bought into the argument that this is a "master-slave" relationship, and that, if the administration do not like this notion, they can find alternate employment. This perceived subservience is fortunately on the wane, but has certainly survived in some municipalities. While the term "master-slave" may not be heard, the attitudes being exhibited certainly convey the same message. Is the administration a respected arm of the local government system, or is it viewed as either unnecessary or at least working at cross-purposes to the governing council?

In our complex environment with challenging requirements, it is fortunate that most people understand why we need to find mechanisms that enable council and its management to work collegially. Quality administrative resources are not readily available. We are not graduating very many skilled and experienced administrators who understand local government. Small municipalities are often faced with looking for what is *available*, as opposed to what is *best*.

Given the challenges of governing and administering, we need a marriage of those keen to lead from a governance point of view and those who are either experienced in administration or willing to learn the nuances of local government. Working in an environment that seeks the best for both is an option. That option, however, may be blessed or inhibited, depending on the choice of governance model.

What Practices Deter Good Governance?

Lack of a critical perspective

Good governance is not reflected by a council that consistently votes unanimously on all the issues. Of course, there may be substantial agreement on many key issues (e.g., the annual budget) and unanimity on those of a housekeeping nature (e.g., passing the minutes). However, presuming that all members of council ought to support the resolution on the floor does not demonstrate either good governance or democracy.

We need to encourage people to think independently. Each councillor was elected with their own point of view, which they carefully articulated to the public during the election process. Taking a group of seven or nine elected officials who each have an independent point of view and presuming that, because they are presented with the same information at a council meeting, they will give a similar response, is faulty thinking. While there is no discernible value in someone being contrary for its own sake, municipalities profit by the exchange of diverse ideas and the challenges that are sincerely expressed.

Assuming the lead role in ABCs

Not everyone I speak with seems to capture this concept, but that has not stopped me from trying to get the message ingrained in their minds. Agencies, boards, and committees (ABCs) are expected to be valuable instruments in their own right because they represent a group of people who tend to support or work together on a particular cause or project. These groups do not need a councillor to be their chair or key spokesperson. That should be the responsibility of one of the other public members (likely the chair).

Members of council are expected to address council issues from the perspective of a community-wide viewpoint. They are not able to do that with any legitimacy if their loyalties have been predetermined according to whatever group or agency they are appointed by council. Being appointed as a council representative in the role of liaison is much different than joining a group as their advocate. Public members appointed to such external bodies often become advocates or begin with a predisposition to its causes. Being an effective councillor is not achievable if being a cheerleader for ABCs is an expected part of the equation.

Becoming an advocate for vested interest groups

Similarly, the spectre of publicly-elected members of council becoming beholden to and speaking on behalf of vested interest groups reduces the credibility and effectiveness of any council. What a councillor represented before being elected to council ought to become part of the history of that councillor, not part of the present. That is, someone who was a member of the ratepayers' group leaves that life behind on election day (and preferably on nomination day), and now represents a much larger audience with sometimes (or often) differing expectations. The advocate for the group to which they used to belong is the chair of that group, which a councillor should never be.

Similarly, someone who was the president of minor hockey leaves that position and perspective behind and takes on one that is far more broadly based and includes the well-being of the community as a whole. Instead of focusing on the availability of ice time for the minor hockey crowd, the focus shifts to "What ice time is available for ringette, figure skating, public skating, minor hockey, and the adult recreation league?" The scale broadens; the audience expands; the point of view is apart from bias; and the community as a whole becomes (or ought to) the sole focus.

Allowing committees to run council

"Governance by committee" is neither legal nor helpful. Allowing or enabling committees to dictate to council what it should decide on an issue takes away from the value of discussion and debate, and presumes that a small number of councillors should be able to direct others on council how to vote. No one on any council loses their opinion or their vote simply because they have not attended a committee meeting. That is not how the system is intended to work.

A committee of council is expected to be a "helper" to council. It can research an issue more fully; seek the input of others external to the council; perhaps understand the nuances of an issue more clearly than others less informed. BUT, it cannot or (at least should not) presume to direct the full council. A committee report is precisely that: a report brought forward reflecting the majority view of the committee members present at that meeting. It may or may not reflect the opinions of the rest of council who, if they were similarly apprised of the issues, may think quite differently. Committees can be a significant help: they are not, however, the legitimate governing body.

Not requiring a full reporting system

Good governance requires that all members of council are equally and concurrently informed. Any system that allows or encourages some members of council to be in the know, while excluding others, runs the risk of creating two classes of councillors. This, in turn, leads to suspicion, which breeds distrust and produces dysfunction. Committees need to report in full to all members of council, not through a verbal report that accomplishes very little, or even through an executive summary. Colleagues on council work best when they understand the full picture. They function poorly when left to guess.

Fascination with the miniscule

Governance is seldom enhanced when councillors are focused on what is "down in the weeds." While there may be items of interest in low-lying places, the best position from a governance perspective is understanding what the view is from the top down. This is not to suggest that what happens on the ground floor is not important; obviously it is. However, if community leaders are to lead effectively, they need to focus on the broad policy aspects – which requires clarity of vision at the top.

What is Executive Policy Governance?

I define Executive Policy Governance as:

> *The leadership of an organization through the conscious policy choices and decisions made by the executive decision makers (both political and administrative) based on a comprehensive, thoughtful policy-based framework.*

This style of governance focuses the key and far-reaching decisions at the senior-most levels of the organization. Governing bodies are elected to make tough decisions and to pass judgment on matters deemed to be beyond the purview of the administration. Further, these decisions are to be carefully constructed based on a comprehensive framework that ensures that all of the key matters are taken into account and judged accordingly.

Why is a new model recommended?

While not every council is struggling with their current model of governance, it seems to me that enough of them are to warrant a fresh examination of the features of a new model and an assessment of whether or not the current model could be improved. Could we find a new model that will capture the best of the current state of affairs and dispense with those elements that detract from good governance?

This model (which permits considerable variation) is based on commonly-accepted principles of good governance and an understanding of how governance functions in a political atmosphere. It respects the distinctive role of the CAO and requires (rather than encourages) a council to stay out of the administrative role, while guiding it carefully through a policy framework and a series of directional purpose statements.

To fully appreciate why a new model is needed, we need to examine what has gone wrong with the current approach to decision making. It is my view that councils meet on a regular basis with little understanding of the important issues facing the municipality and how this meeting will assist in coming to grips with those issues.

Councils also spend considerable periods of time (and thus energy) on aspects of their business that either may not need to be done or could be handled in a much more expeditious fashion. They often find themselves embroiled in heated and prolonged discussion and debates on topics that have already been recently resolved. In addition, debates at the council table are often more focused on the administration than on the consequences of this versus that policy option.

It is often the case that a particular decision may be completely inconsistent with the decision made by this or a predecessor council on a very similar issue. Those affected by the decision are left wondering if they should proceed – knowing full well that the next time the issue is brought to the table, the matter may be resolved quite differently.

Beyond the council chambers, the lack of a policy framework also disadvantages the administration in numerous ways. Decisions may not be implemented quickly, as the administration waits for the next meeting to see if today's decision is to be reversed. Energies may be wasted when the administration *does* act, only to be told to reverse the action. The CAO may refuse to endorse a fairly straightforward matter being proposed by his or her administration for fear of "being burned." Confidence by the public may be lost or at least placed in jeopardy, as the "great decision ball" is punted back and forth down the field, with little discernible progress being made – but considerable resources being expended.

The objectives

What objectives ought to characterize a *new* approach? If the model is to be an improvement over that which presently exists, it will need to:

- ensure that council makes the key governance policy decisions that govern the municipality;
- require of council that it consider on a regular basis the goals, objectives, and aspirations of the community, and that community input be sought on a somewhat regular (i.e., annual) basis, to ensure acceptance of the direction of the council;
- respect the place of a regular council meeting as the primary forum for council decisions, and ensure that the primary business of council is discharged at a meeting of council;
- provide suitable forums for citizen participation on a timely, informed basis;
- provide regular reports to council from any council-established committee, board, or commission;

- at meetings of ABCs, ensure that council members are regarded as *liaison only;*
- require that any actions of ABCs (other than those independently legislated) impacting on the municipality are approved in advance by council;
- place the onus for administrative decisions and advice on the CAO;
- provide council members with the opportunity to reflect on decisions prior to being required to make them;
- place a premium on openness and transparency in the decision-making process;
- ensure that reports of the administration are thorough and independent of political bias;
- ensure that such reports are always coordinated through the office of the CAO;
- enable council to have access to independent counsel from its legal advisor and auditor on a regular basis;
- require council to review and assess the performance of the CAO on a regular, formalized, professional basis; and
- ensure that any personnel-related comments by council are limited to closed door meetings with the CAO.

What are the Key Components and How Does it Work?

While the Executive Policy Governance model will still enable a number of choices to be made by each municipality in terms of how they function from a governance perspective, there are several core elements. Specifically, the model:

- is based on a series of principles, core guidelines, design criteria, and clear policy process (these are central to the effectiveness and impact of the model);
- depends upon council understanding its key powers and the significance of its impact on the organization and the community;
- places an expectation on council to be involved in agenda building;

- provides effective and ongoing mechanisms for effective public participation;
- ensures that council is intimately involved in the policy development process and responsible for executive policy approval;
- strictly adheres to the independence of the administration as an apolitical body with key responsibilities of its own;
- defers additional (albeit modest) "powers" to the role of the mayor, enabling the mayor to better perform the expected duties of office;
- requires a "once per term" public consultation process on community priorities and an annual "review and update of priorities" process involving council, the administration, and a cross-section of key community leaders;
- requires council to be involved annually in a meaningful way with an independent auditor to ensure its fiduciary responsibilities are discharged; and
- requires council to conduct a review of its own effectiveness on an annual basis.

If developed effectively and as described herein, this model will reflect:

- principles of governance that are absolutely central to the model and that council members agree to uphold;
- a series of core guidelines that determine how the model works and link its interdependent parts;
- certain design criteria that speak to how each component adds to the whole;
- council exercising a more "hands on" role in building its meeting agenda, and a more "hands off" role in directing members of the administration; and
- stated annual objectives that are shared with the public, and a "report card" that places the onus on council to provide clear feedback on what has actually been accomplished during the past reporting period (typically the past year).

Template of Interdependent Measures

In addition to the governance criteria, any changes to governance must be considered within a larger framework. That is, if we are proposing changes in one aspect, what *else* needs to be functioning better, in order for the system as a whole to enable council to function at its best?

These proposed changes and improvements include:

➤ improved understanding of council's approach to governance (i.e., council needs to be willing to participate in relevant training in governance matters throughout each council term);

➤ a change in terminology such that council's principal advisor, hereafter is known as the CAO (this term, referencing the chief administrative officer, is generally accepted throughout the municipal sector);

➤ clear understanding of the CAO's role in functioning as council's senior policy advisor and a willingness to follow the protocol of ensuring all administrative advice flows through the CAO (with such a protocol to be written and agreed to, and then adhered to, by council);

➤ a proactive orientation process following each municipal election that places the focus on governance (a policy on orientations should be established now and responsibility designated to the clerk to develop a comprehensive policy and process of orientation);

➤ a proactive approach to strategic planning that ensures council is involved in leading the process on an annual basis, with special attention paid to holding a strategic planning session within 60 days of any municipal election (a policy should be drafted now that reflects this intent);

➤ a renewed commitment and approach to policy development;

➤ a reviewed and potentially revised procedural by-law (depending upon the agreement of council to these governance issues and recommendations);

➤ concurrence on principles guiding the "governance model";

- a governance and priorities committee, with clearly-stated and agreed-upon terms of reference and guidelines;
- an agenda committee formed by the mayor and two members of council (whose role it is to guide the development of policy-oriented agendas, to ensure that council's issues and concerns are being addressed);
- clear guidelines for the work of any staff involved in supporting council's access to information (a council secretariat);
- terms of reference and the provision for a regular rotation of membership on any council-appointed committees;
- a standard "request for decision" format for all administrative reports, in order to improve consistency and ease of identifying the governance issues at stake in any such matter before council;
- clarity about when to employ closed meetings;
- role statements for council, the mayor, and the CAO;
- clearly-defined role for the senior management team in developing policy issues for referral to council and in assisting the CAO to identify administrative versus policy issues; and
- an overall decision-making model and framework to help council and management understand their roles.

The foregoing components form the model that I am proposing. Taken together as an interrelated and interdependent fabric, they will establish your municipality as a leader in municipal governance – and as an organization that is serious about its desire to provide consistent and responsive leadership to residents.

Chapter 8
Foundational Principles and Design Criteria

In the previous chapter, I spoke to the need for a new model, identified its objectives, and described the key components. This chapter details the foundation upon which such a model is founded, setting out a series of core principles that undergird "policy governance" and are designed in such a way as to be interdependent. Design criteria for the new Executive Policy Governance model are then examined.

Foundational Principles

The Executive Policy Governance model is based on the following 10 foundational principles.

1. Accountability to public

Council (mayor and councillors) are elected on behalf of the public as their representatives. As a result, the elected officials are accountable to the public (citizens) in their community.

2. Public input

The input of citizens will always be considered of value to the council. While council may or may not agree with the public's input, it will be taken into account where possible on key governance issues and on other major matters affecting the community.

3. Transparency

The decisions of council will be made at the council table and, unless provided for otherwise by legislation, those decisions will be rendered publicly.

4. Governance role

Council's role is as described in legislation and is most importantly focused on the governance of the community. As such, council will seek to limit its decision making to the policy and planning issues wherein council's decisions are needed to provide the decision with community legitimacy. Council will retain its right to make decisions.

5. Role clarity for elected officials

Council will identify the need for a comprehensive statement that describes in some depth the role of elected officials (including that of the mayor). This description will be grounded in legislation and state the commonly accepted principal roles of a mayor and councillor.

6. Council rights and responsibilities

Council will have the right and responsibility to exercise its independent authority to set forth the community vision (i.e., where are we going from here), the annual and longer-term priorities, governance policies, legislated by-laws, resolutions in council meetings, its governance model, assessment of the CAO, and oversight of the fiscal fidelity of the municipality. While there may be other responsibilities exercised by council, the foregoing are essential to any council adhering to its obligations.

7. Implementation of council decisions

Decisions of council are those that the administration is required to follow. Unless it can be shown to the council (by its clerk or solicitor) that a decision is contrary to municipal law, the decision will be understood as that of the council. The CAO (and the administration) will be expected to implement the decision immediately. That is, regardless of whether there is a division on council relative to the matter, the administration is expected to undertake action on the decisions as expeditiously as though the issue was resolved unanimously.

8. Established protocols

Council will establish "protocols" on matters within its domain that speak to how it does its business. These protocols are to be considered a part of the policy framework of council.

9. Decision-making considerations

The decisions of council will take into account: the anticipated impact on the whole community; any current policy on the issue; the research and advice of the administration; the discussion of council members at the council table; the input of members of the public; any discussion and decision of a committee of council; and the legislation.

10. Policy decision process

Policy decisions of council will be dealt with in a manner distinct from that of simple resolution on a matter. The policy framework of the matter will be presented; the potential impacts will be discussed; and any prior or current related policy will be identified. All policies will be reviewed on a regular basis.

Design Criteria

Will a new or revised model of governance improve how your council governs? On what would you base such a judgment?

In my opinion, council's governance model needs to be structured in such a way that it achieves the objectives as stated, and does so within the context of certain "design criteria." Such criteria might be thought of as "building blocks" upon which the governance model should be established.

A governance model is more than just decision making. The model should reflect what values are important; what objectives are significant; and what results are expected. The model will reflect what each council sees as important. For example, is quick decision making preferred, or is the council content with a more step-by-step (albeit slower) process? Is public input considered desirable, or is it simply to be tolerated? Is council comfortable with the CAO making rather significant decisions, or does council expect to be asked for its opinion on most matters that hit the public's screen?

The design criteria outlined below attempt to address key issues that determine whether or not the model will function as intended, and are the building blocks or foundation upon which the model should be built.

1. Responsiveness to resident needs (public-focused)

Municipalities exist to provide public-focused services to the community. Such services are often largely paid for by the public – residents and businesses – and perhaps, in part, by the province (which also depends upon *its* public for support). As a result, any useful model of governance will be responsive to the expectations of the public and will therefore establish mechanisms of public input. Such mechanisms might be open meetings, surveys, or open houses; or they might be web-based, allowing residents the convenience of providing input from the comfort of their homes.

Being responsive does not simply mean "selling" the decisions of the municipality to its residents. While messaging out is needed and expected, there is also an equal requirement for encouraging input into the decisions of council.

2. Responsiveness to political leadership (accountability)

This criterion points to one of the key underpinnings of local government. The organization's corporate structure and personnel must be responsive to the guidance and leadership of the elected council (a principle known as the primacy of council). Not only must it be responsive to the direction provided by by-laws, resolutions, and policies, but the administration must also have built into it clear levels of accountability. The will of council should be understood as pre-eminent in what decisions are being made, what services are being delivered, how they are being delivered, and how the delivery of services and the expenditure of public funds is being reported and assessed.

Regardless of the delegation of considerable administrative powers to the CAO and his or her staff, the public clearly expects the elected council to be accountable. This requires that council is well informed, engaged in driving the policy priorities, and committed to steering the organization. Within the policy and strategic framework established by council, the administration is charged with making a multitude of decisions that constitute the "rowing" of the organization. Thus, council and the citizenry must be cognizant of who is responsible for administrative action and who, at the end of the day, is accountable for the results.

Within the governance model, council's role in governing the entire community cannot just be generally acknowledged, but must be actually reflected. The model must enable the public to continue to view its elected council as accountable for key decisions.

3. Transparency of decision making (openness)

Public business should be done publicly. This criterion refers to the fact that local governments are expected to function in a far more open environment than either their provincial or federal counterparts. Thus, while some of what a council does must, by necessity, be treated in very strict confidence (largely via closed sessions), there are very few issues that should not be the subject of public debate. These are generally described by either the *Municipal Act* (or Charter) or by freedom of information legislation. These are outlined for good and legitimate reasons and must be respected. (And note that "openness and transparency" does not permit disobeying either the laws or the resolutions of the council, simply because you, as an individual councillor, do not agree.)

Council should make every reasonable effort to ensure that its meetings are made open to the public and, where there is doubt, err on the side of openness (i.e., on the side of the public). Advertise committee meetings; open the doors to preliminary budget discussions; and ensure full agendas are made available to those following online or onsite.

Any governance model worthy of acceptance by the public will embrace transparency. Each council needs to be doing public business publicly.

4. Coordination of resources (collaboration)

Your municipality runs a multitude of "businesses." These "businesses" range from fire services to by-law enforcement, from managing public recreation facilities to offering after-school programs for tots and young mothers, from providing planning services and granting building permits to processing concerns regarding agricultural practices, from engineering and designing new roads to maintaining existing roads. There are, however, numerous areas of overlap – and thus, the potential for duplication. As well, many of these services are interdependent, affecting and even relying upon the actions of other staff in other departments.

Senior management must focus these resources and services in such a way as to minimize the potential for duplication and/or poor communication. These resources are expensive and valuable and must be treated in a collaborative manner. Whatever the governance model employed by council, it must act as an integrator of resources – and not one that contributes to silo management. Functions should be balanced, where possible, in terms of their people, potential impact, degree of complexity, and perceived value to the municipality.

Ensuring that the administrative organization is treated with due care and attention is not your job as elected officials. Your role is to ensure that these management functions get done. That requires council to hire an experienced and effective CAO to oversee the organization; discipline as needed; motivate as much as possible; recruit good people; ensure that they work collegially; and, if necessary, break down any silo thinking.

A governance model that interferes in these managerial processes is quite simply the wrong model. For example, what is referred to as a "portfolio" system or model begs council's interference in the responsibilities of management. Having a councillor sit over an individual department will inevitably produce two department heads, one of whom is elected. This might make the councillor happy, but I will guarantee you that the department head is having difficulty convincing staff that their boss is actually the department head. Whatever else a governance model does, it must support the legislation. The latter typically identifies managerial duties that should not be abridged.

5. Openness to change (flexibility)

The municipal "agenda" is always fluid. That is what makes local government so interesting and generally challenging. It is not possible to deliver an orientation seminar on what decisions to make: rather, the focus needs to be on how to make good decisions. Flexibility is a by-word for the organizational culture of today and, presumably, into the future. As the focus of the business changes over time in response to the perceived needs of residents and businesses, this system must also be open to various kinds of adjustment.

Organizations are dynamic entities. They are not static systems, but rather are as open to change forces as individuals are. Such changes can occur in legislation, the environment, economic factors, demographics, and so on.

To have any hope of standing the test of time, any governance model must, by necessity, be designed with flex built in. If the model is adjustable, the change in issues will be readily addressed.

6. Clarity of authority

Accountability requires specific authority to take action. In order to preserve the respective responsibilities of both council and the administration, the governance model will need to set out the expectations and areas of authority for each party. It must be clear to each part of the organization what duties they are charged with and what level of authority each holds. This clarification is particularly needed and useful in such aspects as:

- authority to make certain decisions;
- power to hire/fire;
- authority to expend funds;
- authority to guide and direct staff; and
- power to advise a political or public body.

The governance model needs to clearly identify who has authority to do what. Those statements might appear in a by-law establishing the position of the CAO or in the terms of reference for a committee; but, regardless, the model should underscore the importance of not violating those requirements and the delegation of duties.

7. Capacity to continue (sustainable)

Not every municipality survives. Sometimes, the fiscal base upon which they have relied collapses; people move away and an already small community becomes marginal at best; the tax rate rises to an unsustainable level; the neighbouring, larger community becomes an attractive home, if for no other reason than financial sustainability.

In the main, however, councils understand that a part of their mandate is to survive. In order to do that successfully, they plan for growth and they plan to tackle areas of liability (for example, aging infrastructure). Council also has a responsibility to ensure that there is a clear succession policy and plan vis-à-vis its relationship to the CAO.

The governance model should be an asset in the search for sustainability. It should be an instrument that supports clear-headed thinking and farsighted planning. In short, it becomes the decision process to ensure that council (and management) think through the future implications of their present day decisions.

8. Simplicity of design (a clear decision-making framework)

The business of a municipality is very complex. Many are involved in a plethora of services and functions, determined in part by legislation and in part by local preference. These services and programs are ongoing commitments that place a tremendous burden on the fiscal and human resource base of the municipality. As a result, the decision-making process needs to be based on the solid ground of quality advice, fiscal realities, a policy framework, and an administration working in concert with its council.

The governance model should not, in any way, add to the complexity of the business; rather, it should enable good decisions to be made in a straightforward manner. Thus, anyone viewing or participating in the conduct of the municipality's business should understand that there is a logical manner by which decisions are made and the work discharged.

9. Currency of information (the right to concurrent advice)

Any system of governance needs to recognize the importance of ensuring access to all policy-related information and subsequent decisions by those who are charged with the responsibility of making policy decisions. This single consideration (i.e., currency of information) augers against any system wherein only certain members have access to the key pieces of information. The notion that only certain members of council are entitled to access information because only they serve on a particular standing committee or board ensures poor governance and a fractured council.

Thus, whatever the governance model, care must be taken to ensure that it enables all members of council to actively and equally share information on a concurrent basis.

10. Concurrent involvement of councillors (equality of members)

The model chosen by council may impact the sense of equality of council members. While few municipalities utilize an "executive committee," wherein certain councillors are deemed to be in the inner circle and thus others in the outer circle, there is the potential for councillors to feel distanced from the decision making. This will happen whenever council establishes a model that enables some members of council to have access to a full briefing on an issue and others to simply receive the minutes of a committee wherein the matter was discussed.

The Executive Policy Governance model is founded on the understanding that all members of council are considered equal and are accorded the respect that should come with elected office.

11. Policy advisory role of the CAO

The mayor and councillors must reinforce the principle of a "one employee" municipality, given that their primary advisor is to be the CAO, and his or her responsibility is to include the guidance, mentoring, and supervision of all other employees. Questions of the administration from council should be directed to the CAO by the mayor or by members of council through the mayor. These should not be directed by councillors to department heads, thus violating this principle. Where the CAO decides, in response to a question by a councillor at a council meeting, to refer the matter to someone else on his or her senior management team, that discretion should be left up to the CAO. This practice will be of considerable help in ensuring that there is respect for this important role and will be likely to help all members of council get off to a healthy start with the CAO.

The governance model needs to embrace the role of the CAO as council's chief policy advisor and ensure that nothing is done that runs counter to that key underlying relationship.

Chapter 9
Understanding Executive Policy Governance

Having argued in favour of a new approach (perhaps only somewhat revised for a few), and having outlined the objectives, principles, and design criteria, let's press on to the core of the model: the policies.

Mechanisms for Council Decision Making

There are essentially three principal mechanisms by which council makes decisions. Resolutions of council reflect the members' view of a particular issue at the moment. In the main, resolutions are not repetitive; that is, they are generally not put before the council to deal with issues that arise frequently. Instead, for the most part, resolutions or motions reflect the will of council regarding topics of a non-recurring nature.

By-laws, on the other hand, are developed and adopted to cover those issues that council feels are of a substantive nature and applicable to all ratepayers, and that may require the power of the courts to ensure compliance and consistency. As well, by-laws are adopted in those areas required by provincial legislation (such as for the borrowing of funds to provide a particular local improvement). By-laws require three readings of council to adopt, and three readings of council to amend or rescind.

The third council decision-making mechanism (and the focus of this book) is that of policy development. Policies are typically developed for those issues that are either of major impact or felt to be repetitive. Thus, policies are not warranted in each instance for every council decision. Instead, policies should be considered if the topic under discussion might be seen to have a significant degree of impact or is one that council might anticipate arising on a frequent basis.

Policy Framework

If this is to be viewed as an Executive Policy Governance model, it is clear that it will only achieve its aims and reflect its name if it embodies a solid core of policies. This is a tricky matter to present and discuss because, while the format and type of content with respect to policies is important, having everyone trying to follow some cookie-cutter model is counterproductive. I do not, for that reason, recommend requesting the policies of other municipalities; the temptation is too great to simply copy those, change the name of the municipality, and replicate the policies. The length of time to undertake that sequence is akin to the duration of impact.

Any council that is interested in *really* making a difference that will last for some time into the future will have a dynamic policy agenda and a refined policy framework.

A policy framework is the centerpiece of the Executive Policy Governance model. Policies must reflect the views of council as the legitimate elected body. Otherwise, they will simply be background reference points at best, or completely discarded (growing mould) at worst. While I understand the concept of administrative policies, those outlined here will largely be targeted at the legislative body (council), because that is where the focus ought to be placed.

What Is Policy?

For the purposes of this book, I define "policy" as follows:

> *A statement of intent, based upon a body of principles or beliefs, approved by the authorized body, that describes what is to be done now and in the future.*

While policies are intended to be followed by the administration and monitored carefully by senior management, they are essentially *guidelines for action based upon a particular intent.* In the main, policies do not describe the detailed actions that are intended to result; they set out a framework within which certain actions are to occur. While policies do not have the legal clout of a by-law, and while they must be approved by council resolution, they are central to whatever action the administration undertakes on significant or repetitive issues. While policies are not written in stone, neither are they cast in jelly. If they are developed according to a carefully prescribed process, policies will be effective guides to the actions that are played out on a daily basis within the municipality.

A thorough process of policy development should generally result in policy statements that are defensible and clearly understood by all parties. Policies should not be quickly cobbled together by the administration and approved by council. Policies are critical to how civic business is done and caution must therefore be exercised to ensure that they are well thought out, with possible consequences identified.

Why Set Policy?

Many municipalities feel that they are sufficiently guided by the prevailing legislation and their own by-laws, and they question the value in setting policy. Sometimes, this is due to a previous experience wherein the policy thwarted what council wanted to do. Or, they may speak of policy as inhibiting council from being flexible in all things (and largely consistent in none).

Policy setting accomplishes a number of objectives.

Policies grounded in a process wherein council is responsible for their approval or change will ***underline the primacy of council***. This is a legislated role of the elected body. Council is the pre-eminent decision-making body, and an effective policy framework will reinforce that concept.

Without thoughtful, balanced policies, the administration is left to scramble for answers to everyday issues in order to provide the public with sound guidance. Policies provide the ***solid foundation for the administration*** to take action. Policies are the "bible" of the administration, in that they provide the authority upon which staff members take action.

Policies *reflect council's perspective on key and repetitive issues*. The administration is able to say, with confidence, "this is the policy of council." The fact that council has adjudicated on the issue and has cast it as a policy shows the intent of the governing body.

Policies provide the authority needed by the CAO and his or her administration to act with confidence, knowing that *council fully supports the decisions of the staff*. Employees will be challenged from time to time about why they took *this* action, rather than that. While sheer logic might be ample justification, the statement that "we are implementing the policy of our council" is a sound response to any question raised by the public.

Policies *provide consistency*. They effectively say "under this or that circumstance, we (the municipality) will do this or that." While they may be challenged in individual circumstances by residents who do not feel that their issue was properly understood, policies establish the basis of decision making and may only be appealed to council for adjustment (or waiver) in a particular and unusual circumstance.

Policies *form the core of how a municipality functions* and upon which it renders decisions. These statements reflect the philosophy and belief system of the elected leaders and the intent that will be illustrated in key decisions. The public often changes the membership of a council at election time because of dissatisfaction with council's policies or its behaviour as a governing body. Generally speaking (albeit not always), major changes are made in council membership when the public senses that the direction council is pursuing is not in concert with the will of the majority of the public. The policy base is important.

Also important is the notion that policies must *reflect the will of this council*. That is, regardless of the fact that a council inherits a policy bank, each successive council must determine which policies it will continue to uphold, which it will change, and any new ones that will be required to reflect the tenor of the new council.

Can Policies Be Changed?

Council members and staff will recognize that policies developed as a result of a thorough process should not be changed frivolously without serious consideration as to whether or not change is justified. A complaint (regardless of how loudly or regularly voiced) may not warrant a change in the policy. But, if the policy is found to not address the issue adequately, its deficiencies will be exposed through daily use and regular commentary. This will lead to changes being made. Circumstances change; a new council is elected that favours quicker growth or fewer restrictions on business (or conversely, more restraints and less growth). The policies must be sensitive to the council of the day.

When council is given the opportunity to see the background decision making that went into current policy, members may well decide that the policy should be supported after all. Thus, while changes to policy are always possible, a rigorous approach to policy development discourages frequent change. Council may, with justification, decide to waive a policy for a particular circumstance or point in time. That does not prohibit council from retaining the policy to deal with future circumstances that were intended or contemplated by that policy.

As a historic example from my own time on council: our city's policy with regard to attendance at the national convention of elected officials (the Federation of Canadian Municipalities) was that the mayor plus two councillors (out of six) were eligible to attend on an annual basis. That seemed to be acceptable, both to the community and to council members. The year that I became FCM president changed the tone. All members felt that they should be able to attend, given the likelihood that such an honour to the community was not to soon be repeated. Our council waived the policy *for that year*. The policy was back in the subsequent year (and, not surprisingly, has since been changed).

Approach to Policy Development

The approach to policy development is almost as important as the results. If council and the administration see providing a broadly-based policy framework as a "one off," then any determination to approach this on a thoughtful basis will almost certainly be doomed.

If there is a great flurry of activity following an election, when the new mayor finds out to his or her horror that the policies central to debate during the election were actually just "the way we do business" – and not policies at all – a push for policies ensues. A task force or committee is struck; members appointed; a deadline may be set; staff are assigned to assist; and expectations rise. Sure enough, within 60 to 90 days, a comprehensive list of policies is presented to council and, with sweeping fanfare, they are approved.

So, what is wrong with the picture? The speed with which those same policies will be forgotten will be equaled by the time taken to put them all together. Why? The process was flawed. Council's ownership of a policy framework will only occur if it fully understood and committed to the policies as they were being presented. That seldom (if ever) happens when a set of policies is approved all at once.

Consider the following case in point. I was asked some time ago to review a not-for-profit organization involved in delivering needed social services at the community level. It offered a wide range of such services and employed capable people to deliver front-line services and programs. When I explored the basis for those services and programs and how they were offered, I asked about the policies that governed them. Few were able to point to the existence of such policies, and yet board members insisted that they did exist. I was sent the document and confess that it contained as comprehensive a set of policies as I have ever seen at the local level.

So, where was the disconnect? Upon examination, I found that virtually all policies were dated the same date. All were new as of that date. The CEO had retained a consultant to assist, and she had fulfilled her obligations to produce executive policies. Other than the CEO and one or two board members, no one else knew what these policies covered.

It is impossible to expect that policies will guide the business of the organization unless they are considered vital to the core of the business. While the aforementioned approach might have produced a good set of policies, they carried little real weight. They needed to be "owned" by the board and administration alike if they were to influence the business of that non-profit.

Planning a Policy Approach

The approach to policy development *must be planned*. This is not akin to turning on the switch, but rather to moving to another home in another community. It takes time to change the current approach and to get it right. If a systematic, sound approach to good governance is to be successful, take the appropriate steps and ensure that all of council is on board.

The following steps should be considered:

- development of the rationale for utilizing a policy approach to decision making;
- preparation of background materials on policy development for the edification of council and administration, ensuring that this material is clearly designated "for council" or "for administration";
- establish training seminars on the topic for both audiences;
- establish an administrative committee to coordinate and steer the process (this body will act as the logistics group, ensuring that the needs of council are being met);
- establish an *ad hoc* council committee to provide leadership to the political or policy aspects of the process; and
- determine what role public participation will play in this process.

Who Does What?

An Executive Policy Governance model is founded on the clear separation of roles. Such a system only works well if both the elected and appointed officials understand their respective parts to be played and refrain from succumbing to the temptation to stray over into the mandate of the other.

The elected council must be in the driver's seat. Council is the body that will ultimately be held accountable for the results or consequences of policies. If these policies are well-received, council may be re-elected. If the policies are felt to be heading the community down the wrong path, new faces around the table are likely.

At the same time, the administration's role is not "second fiddle"; it is simply different. If the model is going to be successful, the administration must be fully engaged in various aspects of preparation and research. Further, whatever policy alternative is accepted by council, the administration will, in most instances, need to be involved in developing the procedural support (i.e., the implementation).

What are the differences in roles?

- Council reviews and approves policy; the administration does not. (I note that there are administrative policies that are folded within the umbrella of council.)
- Council can change its policies or waive them to suit a particular request at that moment; the administration cannot.
- The administration can recommend new policy, but cannot approve policies that lie within council's jurisdiction.
- The administration cannot adjust or waive policies set by council, unless council has approved such changes in advance.
- The administration can seek public input on suggested new policies, but cannot suggest that such policies will ever be approved.
- A new council can decide to change current policies if it finds them to be objectionable; the administration can and should present all current policies to a new council for such a review.

Steps in Policy Development Process

There are certain key steps in the policy governance process. While they will be described in more detail later, these steps include:

- issue identification;
- identification of underlying issues;
- information collection;
- outline of policy alternatives;

- drafting of recommended policy;
- policy adoption;
- policy implementation; and
- policy review and evaluation.

The administration, under the leadership of the CAO, plays a very fundamental role in most of these steps. For instance, the administration can point out, in a report to council, that certain key, underlying issues would indicate the need for a clear policy. Such issues might arise with respect to minor circumstances (e.g., the use of a community hall) or may reflect a much larger issue (e.g., participating in an inter-regional agreement respecting the identification of a waste transfer facility).

The administration can also play a role in researching the matter, to see what underlying issues impact the eventual policy being set by council. Are other policies likely to be affected? Has council ruled on a similar matter recently, wherein a precedent may have been set? Are there likely to be unintended consequences from what is being proposed?

Once any underlying issues related to the policy are unearthed, the administration will also need to seek related information that supports one position or another. What do other municipalities do in similar circumstances? Has this issue been addressed previously by this council or its predecessors? Should the external auditor be asked to provide a comment? Does the issue fall within the scope of legislation impacting municipalities?

If it is a shared responsibility, perhaps with a committee of council, the administration will also likely be called upon to identify the various policy alternatives. For each policy issue, there are likely two or three ways council might wish to proceed. These alternatives may impact the municipality's finances, facilities, personnel – and even its future. Although council may establish an *ad hoc* policy committee of council to become involved at this stage, the administration will still have a role to play in drafting various alternatives and explaining the expected consequences of each approach.

Once the various alternatives have been explored and council (likely through a committee of the whole discussion) has reviewed the options, the administration will be involved in "fleshing out" the recommended policy. I note that, if there is considerable debate in committee on this matter, the administration would be wise to prepare the other alternatives in the same manner. Once council has adopted their preferred choice as policy, then the pursuit of other options is discontinued.

While someone might believe that this would then conclude the work of the administration with respect to the policy process, in some respects it is only getting started. Policies are effective only if implemented. As a result, the role of the administration shifts into a different mode. The procedures that speak to the implementation of policy need to be crafted (some of this work may have preceded adoption of the policy), and that is certainly a role of the administration. I would argue that the less visible that this part of the process is to council, the more likely the separation of council and administration will be respected. While individual members of council may very likely be interested in "how" the policy will be implemented, that is quite simply not their role.

Once policy has been approved and procedures crafted, the policy will be ready for implementation. Again, this is, for the most part, an administrative function – unless it is a governance policy (more on this later), in which case the implementation may only concern council. As a relatively straightforward example, if council approves a policy of permitting councillors to attend conferences of their choosing, up to a maximum of $2,500 per year, the implementation will be councillors attending conferences. Admittedly, some of the procedures will still impact administration (i.e., completing the required paperwork).

So, now we are finished, right? Wrong. Policies are only truly effective if they are subject to ongoing review and evaluation. Is the policy achieving what it was intended to do? Have there been unintended consequences that the framers of the policy might not have contemplated? Could the policy be tweaked somewhat to remove the problems that have been cited? Has the policy led to the need for a larger policy, or exposed the absence of a much larger policy? All of the above may have been encountered, but infrequently. It may not make the current policy inadequate, but rather the starting point of a broader discussion.

What's the Result?

Why the push to get councils to really bear down on establishing a rigorous approach to policy development? From a council perspective, what are the expected results of such an approach? What about from the perspective of the administration?

IF the approach is well thought out, and IF the approach is inclusive of the steps outlined in this chapter, THEN the following should be expected.

Improved clarity of roles – Council's authority in setting policies and management's role in carrying them out should be readily identified and respected.

Enhanced clarity of messages – Council should be able to articulate a new course of direction within a policy framework and be assured that its message of change is being implemented expeditiously and within the context of council's revised direction.

Consistency of responses – Council will be able to rely on its administration to be absolutely consistent in how it responds to concerns and queries by the public. If the policy is clear, this will direct the response. Regardless of who asks, the response is the same. If the person persists in seeking a change to the policy, the path to council's door is outlined.

Delegation of duties – Once the policy has been articulated, the CAO and his or her senior administration can confidently delegate the tasks to be done with a clear recognition that these duties have already met the approval of council. The flow of communication is improved; performance can be assessed; results can be evaluated.

Uncertainty is reduced – Effective policy making reduces uncertainty. The administration is made aware of council's intent; procedures are crafted; steps to implement the policy are drafted by the administration; and work is carried out in an atmosphere of trust and certainty.

Business planning and budgeting processes are enhanced – Council's policies should set the direction of a good business planning and budgeting process. The administration is armed with an understanding of current policies, as well as the results of council's annual goals and priorities exercise. This powerful combination will facilitate effective planning for the future.

Council's primacy as decision maker is enhanced – Central to an effective governance model is the creation of a policy framework that ensures the primacy of council is reflected in all key decisions impacting the direction of the community and civic organization.

Impact on Governance Model

Executive Policy Governance, as its name implies, relies to a significant degree on the understanding of council that its policy-setting role should never be overlooked nor taken for granted. This model requires the administration to approach every issue from a policy perspective. Each topic on a council agenda is prefaced by the question:

> *What current policy is affected, or what policy is being proposed or recommended for change?*

It may be that the administration is not proposing any change. The issue may be on the agenda because, in the opinion of the CAO, the topic is important and the continued implementation of the current policy by the administration may no longer be warranted. Conditions do change, and sometimes dramatically. Or, there may be a significant public outcry regarding council's current or recently-established policy, and the CAO wisely believes that council needs to be made aware of these concerns. Perhaps legal counsel has subsequently been sought and is recommending certain changes in the policy statement.

The advantage of such an approach is a "raising of the governance bar," such that the real role of council is its central focus. It is too easy to be moved away from this role and to focus on all the trifling

Chapter 9 • Understanding Executive Policy Governance

matters that take time, but do very little to establish and support the important focus of council.

Consider this case in point:

The council of a reasonably large municipality felt that it should hold regular meetings on a weekly (rather than bi-weekly) basis, given their lengthy agendas and the sense of always being rushed to "get through" them. The meetings invariably ran well past the closing hour as stated in the procedural by-law, and major decisions were often being considered when the rest of the community was either in bed or watching the last moments of the national newscast.

When the administration and council struck an *ad hoc* committee to review what alternatives were available beyond simply meeting more frequently (which was not recommended by the administration), they found that the notion to meet every week was largely predicated on the knowledge that, without longer or more frequent meetings, the "big" agenda items would not be addressed.

Besides numerous other changes that this review entertained, one of the councillors asked the seemingly harmless question, "Why do we go through the correspondence and have it read aloud at the start of each meeting?" Now, for some readers, this may sound foreign or ludicrous. It should be, but it isn't. I have sat through countless meetings wherein the clerk rises to read the correspondence (or at least those items deemed to be of some significance by the clerk). This is followed by an outpouring of questions by individual members of council who want to either assure the public that they are concerned with every issue, or be quoted with a "public service" response to the question or issue raised. When the mayor finally tires of the spectacle and feels that it has been milked for all it is worth (and then some), he asks for a motion to refer these matters to the CAO for a response.

The whole process could have been significantly improved if:

➤ "correspondence" was removed from the agenda;
➤ the words "policy implications" prefaced each administrative report;

- ➤ no item was to be placed on a council agenda unless accompanied by a "request for decision," as drafted by the administration; and
- ➤ both council and administration realized that the current practice wastes everyone's time and actually acts to undermine the responsibility of the administration to act as advisors, not as readers.

Chapter 10
Taking Action within a Decision-Making Framework

Council should, by policy, establish a decision-making framework. This would eliminate any process that does not comply with the policy as set by council. Executive Policy Governance relies on a thoughtful process of decision making that should never be compromised by short-circuits, wasted processes, useless activity, or any action that undermines the fidelity of the process and council's intentions.

Decision-Making Framework

What does such a process look like? It contains the following key elements.

Council

- review of reports and recommendations;
- discussion of policies;
- approval of motions, resolutions, by-laws, policies; and
- final authority within legal limitations.

Committee of the Whole

- review of status reports;
- review of proposed new policies;
- discussion of status updates on requests by councillors for information; and
- power to advise.

CAO

- review of senior staff requests;
- review (and approval) of tenders, purchases, budgets;
- review of staff performance;
- preparation of advice to council; and
- decision-making powers as defined by by-law.

Senior Management Group

- review of departmental matters;
- coordination of work with other departments;
- advice to the CAO; and
- discussion of background reports, council requests, etc.

Executive Policy Governance relies extensively upon clarity of roles. Council needs to understand its part in the process. The CAO and management team similarly want clarity as to what council needs from them in order to make the decision making clear and credible. If a committee system is employed (either a standing committee model or a committee of the whole), then the role of the committee must also be made clear.

Policies and the Planning Process

Good policy development flows from a comprehensive matrix of issues, plans, budgets, prior decisions, change in council make-up, new circumstances, change in legislation, etc. There is, of course, more than one type of policy and more than one approach to policy making.

Municipalities are encouraged to view policy development as one step on an overall continuum of developing thoughtful responses to local issues. Thus, policies should be seen as one of the natural outcomes of a much broader, hierarchical planning process.

Regardless of what approach is taken, however, council should ensure that it is grounded in a policy framework. So ... a new council takes office, and some wise soul suggests that council place its stamp upon the community and the organization by creating its own mission and vision statements. Before jumping in, ask the question: What is our policy in this regard? My suspicion (based on some experience) is that you will not find one. So, create it. What is the policy of our new council? It could be something as simple as "The council of XYZ Community will discuss and determine its mission and vision within 60 days of each municipal election." That simple statement is a policy, complete with intent and timing. It cannot be bypassed (although it could be voided by any subsequent council). In other words, the administration of the day would be required, by this policy statement, to bring the matter before council right after an election and ask: "What is the will of this council? One of your predecessor councils thought that this policy made a lot of sense. Is it your wish to follow up on this and consider our mission and vision? We find that there has been considerable merit to having this discussion."

And Again, Policy Leads to Action

If the policy outlined above is implemented, it may be useful to add on a chapter or two. Thus, the council may wish to also develop its goals and priorities, concurrent with the vision and mission. These additional items fall naturally from such a policy and add immeasurably to the sense of direction and cohesion of council and its administration. The resulting process (outlined in the table below) also leads naturally to a full discussion of budgets and available funding. All of these are policy issues.

Step-by-Step Process	Description
Mission Statement	Overall outline of mandate of municipality.
Goal	Broad, future-oriented statements of direction.
Specific Objectives	Specific, measurable outputs and targets.
Strategies	Techniques and resources for achieving the objectives.
Policies	Statements of intent describing what is to be done.
Procedures	Statements or regulations describing who does what, how, and in what sequence.

Types of Policies

Policies reflect council's view of what is to be done in order to achieve its aims and objectives. Such policies may be part of a broad, long-term planning process, or they may be much more specific in response to a particular circumstance.

Using a descriptive hierarchy or framework, policies may be categorized as follows.

Policies of intent – Policies of intent are those that are broad-based and deal with long-term issues, reflecting the intention of council to take certain actions on the goals and priorities of the community. For example:

> *The council of _____ recognizes the importance of joint council-staff input to priority setting and budgeting, and thus will hold an annual corporate strategy retreat to discuss and set goals and objectives.*

Situational policies – Situational policies refer to those policies established by council in response to a particular circumstance or occurrence that may not have been foreseen in the course of normal decision making. For example:

> *The council of _____ will provide administrative assistance to all individuals whose properties suffered flooding damage during the recent flood, by assisting in the preparation of insurance and damage claims; and by directing staff to assist in the pumping out of residential basements on a "no liability" basis.*

Routine policies – Routine policies are those that are drafted in response to ongoing issues or to issues that may be anticipated in advance (i.e., a proactive response). For example:

> *The coat of arms for the regional district will be confirmed as shown in the attached illustration marked as Exhibit A.*

> *The council will reimburse the costs associated with registration and attendance at relevant seminars and courses for*

any employee, provided that the employee has received the prior approval of his or her supervisor.

Administrative policies – Administrative policies are those that deal with day-to-day issues falling within the mandate and authority delegated to the CAO. For example:

A labour-management committee consisting of the CAO and Director of Corporate Services, together with two representatives of CUPE, will meet on a monthly basis to review ongoing issues as they arise, as per the attached terms of reference.

Approaches to Policy Making

Policies can result from a variety of circumstances and origins. These range from a defined step-by-step process to other, more *ad hoc* ways of developing policy. Previous "unwritten" policy may be cited; amendments may be made to an existing policy after some review and research by staff; new policies may be brought forward by staff or committees; or an existing policy may be changed by council on the spur of the moment.

Regardless of these variations, the following two principal types of approaches appear paramount. These are:

Rational policy making – defined as a step-by-step approach to developing policies through which various alternatives are reviewed and evaluated prior to the "best" policy being approved.

Incremental policy making – where existing policies are added to or subtracted from, and are seen as the basis upon which a new policy might be constructed.

Rational policy making presumes that the drafters of policy are beginning with a blank slate and no fixed preconceptions of how the policy should appear. With such a mandate, the administration is thus empowered to consider all available options, regardless of how extreme or innovative they might be. This process inevitably results in a series of useful options, with the administration's "best" policy being placed before council for approval.

Council members are then at liberty to decide if the best solution as proposed by administration is in agreement with what "fits" the best from their own political perspective. On the other hand, incremental policy making can also produce good results. An existing policy may be found somewhat deficient for the changing circumstances, but the basic policy structure might be viewed as a useful "straw man" on which to hang a new policy. Policies can therefore emerge from a series of small steps or alterations to an existing policy, rather than from a new approach. As a result, some authorities argue that the conservative nature of locally-elected officials leads to only minor variations to the current "way we do things."

Both approaches are possible and workable, however, depending on the current situation and the philosophy of each council and its administration. The preferred approach is the "rational" one, in that it forces the administration and council to review each policy in a logical sequence. Once policies have been established, simple amendments from time to time may be all that is required to bring the policy more in line with the thinking of the present council.

The end result of the process is a formal resolution of council adopting the recommended policy. Such a step, however, should not occur until such time as each recommended step has been covered. The final decision-making authority with regard to the adoption or denial of policies rests solely with council. So, while council might have any number of bodies involved in researching and drafting policies, it still remains up to council to decide whether or not the policy meets its approval. As a result, council has the ultimate authority in approving individual policies.

Roadblocks to Executive Policy Governance

Good governance relies upon the establishment of effective, timely policies. While it might seem to be logical that all governing bodies will want to be on top of this and will embrace policy governance, there are many who do not. In each instance, different arguments (explored below) might be heard as to why a more flexible, spontaneous approach is supported.

"We've always done it this way"

Perhaps the most frequent argument heard is that of "it has always been done this way before." Certainly, tradition can seem like an imposing barrier to making change. Members who are accustomed to dealing with all issues on a resolution basis may therefore find it difficult to understand why some of those issues should be dealt with through policy. Overcoming this barrier takes time and patience, together with opportunity, in order to demonstrate to council the real benefits of policy making.

It should be remembered that "the way we have always done it before" may indeed constitute current policy. That is, if there is a motion in the council minutes from a previous meeting authorizing a certain action to be taken, that resolution comprises the existing policy. What is done now is the basis of a new policy. The difference is one of approach: a policy development approach requires that a step-by-step review be undertaken prior to passing the necessary motion; a simple resolution, on the other hand, may be passed at any duly called meeting, without this more planned process being utilized.

All decisions require a policy

A second barrier to real policy development is the perception by some that, once policy work is introduced to the organization, all subsequent decisions must be made via the policy process. This, of course, is simply not true. Most council decisions will continue to be made by a simple motion or resolution. On the other hand, those issues that are major and that appear to be repetitive should be dealt with through policy.

Lack of understanding

A third roadblock to policy development has been the absence of training. It is one thing for conference leaders to talk about the need for policy development ... and quite another to provide training for those affected. Members of senior staff and council should be introduced to policy governance through training sessions, so that they see the value of using a step-by-step process to develop policies.

Policies protect the administration

The fourth roadblock to policy development can be the perception (often by some members of council who sit on other agencies and boards where policies are used regularly) that senior staff have a tendency to hide their action or inaction behind existing policy. In other words, policies are made to seem impervious to change. Regardless of the fact that they are established by policy makers, some organizations have given the perception that staff are controlling the decision-making process and are resisting any efforts to change current policy.

A Continuous Process

Policy development is an ongoing process. Issues arise or are expected; responses are required by council; and policy statements may be needed. Alternately, current policies may be challenged and deemed to be unsuitable. As a result, changes may be needed.

Certainly, not all necessary policies can or should be drafted at once. While it may be possible to outline various policy topics at the outset, it is not desirable to see policy development as a "big bang" or "one shot" event. Policies need to be approached carefully and thoughtfully – preferably one at a time.

If the process is being initiated for the first time, it is likely that council will want to address a number of policies fairly quickly in order to show that it is committed to this more progressive way of decision making. Some of these may be based on new issues, while others will be the result of unwritten policies being finally and formally committed to in writing.

Policy making is analogous to a new, living organism that requires constant attention in order to grow and to fully develop. Not all growth nor all policies occur at the same time. Like the development of any organism, policy making can be unpredictable and erratic. A series of policies may be written at the outset, followed by individual policies presented every meeting or so. There may well be times when no new policies are required, as the key basic issues have been addressed. And yet, at other times, a major issue might be discussed that requires a new policy to be developed.

For instance, council may undertake a comprehensive review and updating of the transportation plan, which may result in a series of new policies. Policies are not to be developed and then promptly forgotten. The policies themselves will cause certain actions or steps to be taken. The administration must view policies as a part of the network defining what responses are appropriate from that point on with respect to questions or actions covered by that policy.

Policies thus anticipate action, and they require constant vigilance to ensure that the will of council is being properly attended to at all times.

Chapter 11
Establishing a Policy Framework

Executive Policy Governance works well if the resulting policies are placed in an overall context and viewed as the core element of a much larger picture. While I have consistently argued that the policy statement itself should be brief, there is considerable value in developing some context surrounding the policy, in order to give it real meaning.

My intent in all of my writing has been to create the basis for a healthy dialogue. Perhaps your municipality is already following a solid, comprehensive model that may, in fact, be further ahead of where this model lies. For many others, however, this model is quite new, and should be seriously considered. If you are a new councillor, recognize that most good innovations start with newcomers. Why? The folks who were elected this past term (or previously) hate to admit that they did not get it all right the first time! So, ask the question: What model do we use – or is there one? Do we just approach all issues as though this community was experiencing this for the first time? Do we need to wait for a natural disaster to ask if we have an emergency plan in place that takes all recognized risks into account? What is our policy?

In order for this new, renewed, or revised policy development approach to "take flight" and add real value to the governance of any community, it must be viewed in an overarching context. When this is seen as a "one off," it quickly loses its currency and council will revert back to the way it has always done business. That outcome is not healthy for either council or the administration.

A "policy framework" provides an envelope or broad umbrella to the process and ensures that issues are viewed in their proper perspective. What should such a framework look like?

Example: The XYZ Policy

A. The Issue

This section of the policy should describe the issue that the policy is intended to address. What aspects of the governance system need to be addressed? What context enables the reader to better understand why this policy is being promulgated? The municipality exists to deliver services to its residents. It attempts to do so in a cost-effective and efficient manner. Its objective of being open and transparent requires that it act in certain ways.

In other words, this section should help the reader to understand events that led to this policy being considered.

Consider the example of a municipality that was working through its policy development process, with a view to adjusting how policies were considered by council. One of the issues discussed was "succession planning." This resulted in the following being drafted:

> The well-being of ABCD County rests upon the capacity that it has to govern effectively and to deliver effective, efficient, and desired services. This capacity relies upon, in some measure, the ability of the county to identify quality candidates for elected office and to provide them with the training and orientation they need to be effective in their roles as public representatives. It also requires that the county is cognizant of its role and responsibilities in:
>
> ♦ structuring the organization so as to best provide the services it wishes to deliver to its citizens;
> ♦ ensuring that the services and actions of the administration take into account the goals and objectives of the council;
> ♦ ensuring that the human resources needed to deliver those services is present in the organization and sufficiently skilled

to handle the challenges of an ever-changing environment; and

* providing the leadership resources needed by a growing workforce, so as to ensure that they are motivated, learning in their roles, held accountable for quality performance, and delivering services in such a manner that the citizens are satisfied with the effort and responsiveness shown.

While these are challenges facing the entire organization and for which the council is held accountable, the focus of council's responsibility lies in its relationship to its CAO. The council is aware that it must carefully manage this relationship in such a manner that it engenders respect and enjoys the mutual trust so essential to this interface. It is also aware that there is a demand for quality people employed in this senior level position, and that this CAO may either leave to take on another position elsewhere or may retire early. As a result, the council must ensure, as a matter of good governance, that it develop both a succession policy and plan for the position of CAO.

B. Mission, Vision, Values

Secondly, it is helpful to build the case for the policy by placing it within the context of the municipality's mission/vision/values statement. In many instances, the policy will add emphasis or meaning to the mission statement. These statements could be set out separately in the policy framework or identified on their own.

In the example cited above, the municipality's vision, values, and core business are stated as follows:

Mission

To enhance the quality of life for people within ABCD County through the efficient and effective use of available resources.

Vision

ABCD County is a desirable community in which to live and do business.

Core Values
- economical and efficient services;
- sound financial management;
- long-term planning;
- a lifestyle of choice in safe communities;
- quality infrastructure; and
- effective leadership.

C. Related Organizational or Strategic Goals

The third section will address how the proposed policy fits with the municipality's strategic or organizational goals. What is the municipality attempting to do that will be impacted by this proposed policy? How will the policy impact the organization? Will the structure be affected? Staff? The human resources environment?

Related Strategic Goals
- *to become the "employer of choice" in this region;*
- *to create a work environment that allows our municipality to attract the best employees; and*
- *to be able to replace any planned absences adequately and to replace any unplanned absences from within the organization.*

Related Organizational Goals
- *to attract first class employees and ensure they are given access to developmental opportunities;*
- *to ensure that the comprehensive human resource needs of the organization are consistently being identified and addressed;*
- *to update the human resource needs on a regular basis;*
- *to identify internal candidates for possible promotion into more senior level positions; and*
- *to ensure that the organization consistently identifies training opportunities that enhance the ability to develop such candidates.*

D. Definition

The fourth main aspect to cover is the definition of terms. What does the policy mean? This is a critical issue to resolve, so that someone reading the policy three years later will still be able to judge what is intended and what the terms mean. Some words take on different meanings over time, and thus, in the absence of definitions, what we thought was clear today may not be so evident in later years.

So, for example, if the policy deals with the topic of "succession planning," the definition might sound something like:

> ***Succession planning*** *is a process of identifying future successors to key positions in the organization. It is part of a broad process of reviewing organizational requirements, identifying the essential skills needed for all key positions, and ensuring that management development programs are established or pursued to ensure that such skills are being developed.*

E. Linkage to Other Council Documents

This considers whether the policy might also be linked to other key municipal policies or council-approved documents. So, for example, a policy on succession planning will likely be linked to one on recruitment. If so, a reference should be made in the policy document that makes that connection:

> *The Succession Policy is but one of a series of inter-linked policies and strategies that will ensure that ABCD County continues to be recognized as an "employer of choice." This policy is also directly linked to council's recruitment policy (see Policy #1234) and recruitment plan for the position of CAO.*

F. The Policy Statement

The foregoing sections place the policy statement in a proper and understandable context, answering questions about why the council is doing this; the context of the policy; how it links to other fundamental aspects of the municipality; and its importance. The actual policy might then sound something like this:

> *The council of ABCD County believes in the importance of its employees to the welfare of its citizens. Council understands that its employees are essential to enabling citizens to enjoy this municipality and its many benefits, including all of the services rendered by the county. Council respects the authority it has vested in its CAO, and thus realizes that council guides the organization through the CAO. As a result, council is responsible for ensuring that it has a plan in place to ensure an orderly transition from one CAO to another whenever that needs arises. The succession plan is based on council's desire that the organization continue to function in a responsive manner, despite any changes in administrative leadership, and particularly during a transition period when council is in the process of recruiting a new CAO.*
>
> *In the absence of its CAO, council's policy is: that it will ensure the appointment of an interim CAO; that the succession plan is followed; that council is afforded the time and resources necessary to ensure that the best candidate for any vacant CAO position is identified; and that the future needs and aspirations of the county, as council understands these to be, will be a part of any decision as to a replacement for the outgoing CAO.*

Chapter 12
Developing a Policy Mindset

It will occur to you that policies are the result of issues arising – and issues are the result of human behaviour. This observation is likely to continue as long as civilization does. If you try to anticipate all of the policy issues now, or if you fall into the well-worn trap of trying to impose a neat and tidy system that has them all created for you, you will be disappointed (but hopefully not surprised).

Should Every Municipality Possess the Same Policies?

While one could argue that local government in each province and state across North America is at least largely the same within that specific jurisdiction (which is at least partially true), it is still apparent that issues are often quite different and will be responded to in varying ways. "Cookie cutter" policies may appear neat and tidy, but they seldom have any lasting impact, unless they have been constructed by the local council and administration in response to current circumstances.

Having said that, there are some key underlying issues that are "generic" to all municipalities. For example:

➤ What is our policy regarding adopting a policy mindset?
➤ What is our policy on setting council priorities at least once annually?
➤ What is our policy on "one employee"?
➤ What is our policy on reviewing our CAO on a regular basis?
➤ What is our policy on ethical behaviour? On adopting a council code of conduct?

- What is our policy on access to administrative advice?
- What is our policy on governing in the best interests of the whole community?
- What is our policy on access to public input?
- What is our policy on access to the external auditor? To other external specialized advice?
- What is our policy on attendance by councillors at meetings of agencies, boards, and committees?
- What is our policy on adhering to a strict interpretation of respect for confidentiality?

These are policies of intent that ought to form the backdrop or context for addressing other policy issues as they arise. Should these be worded the same as our neighbour's? Likely not. In many instances, each municipality is (or should be) distinct. Will there be parallels? Quite likely.

Categories of Policies

Are policies needed on all issues? No. Are they useful on key, ongoing issues? Absolutely!

The issues that a council will face over a term are not readily definable, nor do they necessarily fit into ready-made chapters. They can, however, be grouped into sections that capture the major elements or categories, based largely on the spheres of jurisdiction established by legislation in your province. While I would argue that every community can (and possibly should) establish its own "policy categories," the following outline suggests what I believe the categories *could* be:

1.0 Council Governance

2.0 Council Leadership & Organization

3.0 Compensation & Expenses

4.0 Internal & Inter-Municipal Relationships

5.0 Council-CAO Relationship

6.0   Departmental/Operational Policies

7.0   Environmental Issues

8.0   Economic Development

9.0   Risk Management

10.0 Emergency Planning

11.0 Agencies, Boards & Committees

12.0 Other

Statements of Protocol

There may be also value in developing a series of "protocols" to define and add weight to this policy envelope. These protocols speak generally to how council and its administration agree to function as the two halves of the same organization, and govern how members of council and the administration will behave in oft-repeated circumstances. These could also potentially (and alternatively) be policy statements. Protocol issues may include the following:

- concurrent information;
- advice to the council;
- relationship to city manager and management;
- treatment of senior administration;
- primacy of policy;
- requests for information;
- public profile;
- appreciation of democracy;
- respect for each other in chambers;
- obligation to inform; and
- diversity of views.

For example, a protocol on concurrent information may state:

> *Any request by a council member to the administration for additional information on an issue to be presented to council that warrants a response by management will be circulated to each member of council concurrently.*

A protocol on advice to council may stipulate:

> *Any advice presented to council in writing or orally by the CAO or by a member of the administration will be received with respect by the council, regardless of whether or not such advice is adopted by council.*

Impact of Agenda Building on Policy

In the context of a municipal council, there are two uses for the word "agenda." The first refers to council's broad agenda of what it sees as being important to accomplish. The second refers to the itinerary for meeting: i.e., council's meeting agenda. This section refers to the latter term.

In my opinion, the "agenda" is core to council. It is an "itinerary of decision making," setting out: what decisions are needed; what information council needs to hear; and who council will hear. Some of its content is established by legislation (i.e., this is what must be decided by council) and some by practice (i.e., this is what we, as the administration, believe council should be discussing and determining at this meeting).

It seems odd that the "council agenda" is so named when, in fact, it might be best referred to as "the administration's idea of what this council should be made aware of and decide at this time." This is rather a long title, but you get the idea. In many municipalities, the meeting agenda is often wholly put together by the administration and then circulated to council. Some of this is to be expected in that there are some issues that do require the approval of the council, such as by-laws, hearings, and plans, and must thus appear on the agenda.

But, should the administration be fully responsible for the actual agenda? I would argue not; that there is a role for the council (or a portion thereof) to fulfill. Such a role must be carefully designed so that any potential for abuse is addressed and preferably mitigated. The proposed instrument for doing so is an "Agenda Committee."

The Agenda Committee mandate (see Chapter 14 for a broader description) is to ensure that council has a direct hand in guiding what goes on its meeting agendas, and thus ensuring that the *key policy matters* are always brought before council. The committee's job is to review all matters suggested for the next agenda and determine the priorities, ensuring that council's requirements and its "agenda" (per the other definition referenced earlier) are being appropriately recognized. The intent would be a blending of the three main aspects of an agenda: the issues that legislation dictates must be decided by council; those issues for which the administration believes the direction of council is needed; and those issues that council wants to see addressed (and which may reflect more of council's own priorities).

Ensuring a Model Based on Policy Governance Approach

A second key route for ensuring council leadership in deciding what should be debated may be achieved through what is commonly referred to as a "committee of the whole" (COW). A COW is not a reference to a closed meeting of council; it simply refers to council as a whole body meeting as a *committee,* and not in a formal process or setting as a council. A committee is intended as an advisory, thinking process; a council meeting is a more adversarial setting, wherein recommended decisions are debated and decided.

The *advantages* of the COW model are as follows:

➤ all of council is concurrently informed and involved; no one member or group of members has more access to power or information than another;

➤ enables council's focus to be geared toward policy issues;

➤ the administrative analysis and advice can readily be orchestrated through the CAO's office;

➤ all of council can participate in the policy debates;

- allows policy issues to be surfaced at this step, and thus provides for a time of reflection prior to formal consideration at council; and
- allows for a more informal discussion between members of the public and council, and allows for greater flexibility in applying time constraints.

The perceived *disadvantages* of such a model are:

- these meetings can become a dress rehearsal for council meetings, so that the importance of a council meeting is diminished; council may choose to simply ratify committee of the whole decisions at the next regular meeting of council;
- the focus is necessarily on the important and broad issues, thereby deterring councillors from becoming involved in lesser issues;
- the agenda can become the sole domain of the CAO, such that councillors may find it difficult to get their own "agenda" items heard;
- the opportunities to view the performance of department heads may be less than in a standing committee system; this makes any assessment of department heads by council more difficult, and thus any succession planning is thereby inhibited; and
- the opportunities for public involvement in close proximity to a policy-setting forum are limited to this meeting, plus that of regular meetings of council.

Solid policy development is most likely to emanate from a committee process, preferably committee of the whole. However, because of the identity/purpose issues surrounding the COW terminology, it may be helpful to think of it (and refer to it, as I have below) as a "Governance and Priorities Committee."

The purpose of the governance and priorities committee (GPC) is to enable members of council to discuss significant agenda issues with the administration in a non-confrontational environment prior to the presentation of such matters as action issues on a council meeting agenda. The GPC is not expected to make any key decisions, as that role should be reserved to a regular meeting of council. The value of a GPC meeting (open to the public) lies in its purpose, which is a forum (for council members and the administration) to present and discuss the more consequential policy issues. These are the issues that have a broader impact on the overall council agenda (i.e., its priorities) and should thus be explored in a setting that lends itself to discussion, rather than resolution.

A GPC meeting is not intended as a decision-making meeting. It is intended as a meeting to: flesh out the key issues; have a thorough discussion of the options; hear from any related experts if so desired; and then move the matter to the next council meeting for a resolution. Otherwise, the council meeting simply becomes a rubber-stamping mechanism.

GPC meetings function at their best when the focus of the agenda is on the key policy issues of the day. A surprise flood in part of the community may be a disaster. Analyzing it and then doing nothing is a tragedy. What policy did we have in place? What failed us in this flood? Had we properly thought through all of the possible scenarios? Do we have a policy of relocating affected families, even if only on a temporary basis? Do we have a policy of providing some form of temporary assistance to those who have lost their homes, businesses, and perhaps even their properties? What does our risk management policy say? When did we last review it?

GPC meetings will generally have both a public and private component. Issues in the latter category would largely be restricted to legal matters, confidential land purchases and sales, and personnel issues (or other similar matters incorporated within privacy legislation) and/or as advised by the municipality's solicitor.

Chapter 13
Importance of Council Meetings

It is interesting to note that the importance of the forum for making final decisions on behalf of the municipality is often overlooked. Some approach council meetings with a *laissez-faire* attitude, giving little thought to how important such meetings are (or at least could be). Council meetings are critical to the decision-making process, as it is at these meetings that final decisions are rendered. As a result, careful thought should be given to their planning, intent, procedures, and follow-up action.

Council meetings ought to be held as needed, and not as a matter of history (i.e., wherein council may meet every one to two weeks). If there are no significant issues worthy of a meeting, then postpone the meeting. The notion that meetings must be held as a sort of religious practice makes it seem as though the meetings are legislated. They are only required insofar as council has these noted in the procedural by-law. If the meetings *are* essential, is there evidence of this fact in terms of administrative and council preparation? Is each issue clearly identified as a policy topic or at least something that requires council's authorization? Is there an administrative report that serves as a backgrounder to every topic on the agenda? Has the report been verified by the CAO as clear, comprehensive, and focused – and one on which he or she has signalled concurrence? Has council consulted with management on the need for meetings every one to two weeks? (Holding meetings weekly is a sure recipe for council to become inordinately involved in "administrivia.")

Meetings of council are intended to not only enable council to "get its business done," but also to provide the public with an opportunity to view the process and participate where desired or possible.

Key Procedural Matters

The following items are among the essential components that should be incorporated into council's procedural by-law:

- purpose and timing of council's regular meetings (which should generally occur every two to four weeks, unless the need for such meetings indicates otherwise);
- purpose and timing of any committee of council meetings (which should generally occur on a date separate from a meeting of council, thereby permitting the administration time to prepare the report for council's attention);
- reference to an agenda for all such meetings – which agenda should NOT be included in the procedural by-law, to ensure that any minor changes may be made without requiring by-law changes (i.e., the agenda should be attached as a policy document that can be amended much more readily than a by-law);
- purpose and timing of any closed meetings; the legal requirements for same;
- attendance at all meetings, particularly noting the role (and right) of the CAO in determining which management staff members (other than the clerk and solicitor) should be in attendance at committee or council meetings;
- the right of the mayor to *briefly* comment on any matter before council as the closing speaker (without vacating the chair), indicating his or her support for or opposition to the matter – and the reasons – prior to calling the vote;
- the timing of delegations, such that they might be heard without being rushed; and specifying that a briefing will be sent to all such delegations prior to any meeting at which they are scheduled to appear to provide clarification around procedural rules governing how delegations present to council;
- the fact that no decision will be made by council with respect to a delegation's request at the time the delegation is heard for the first time, unless the delegation has provided a dossier on the issue at least 10 days prior to the regular meeting of council;

Chapter 13 • Importance of Council Meetings

➤ that correspondence addressed council will be circulated to all members of council in advance of meetings of council; and that, unless deemed by the agenda committee to be important to the community, the item will not appear on the council agenda;

➤ that business items received by the office and requiring a response from council will be presented to council at its next regular meeting, together with a covering report on the matter by the CAO;

➤ that councillors may place items on the agenda to be considered by the agenda committee: if the matter addresses a current policy that a councillor wishes to appeal, it will be placed on the next council agenda as is; if it is not a matter addressed by a current policy of council, it will be referred to the CAO, who will prepare a report on the matter for council at its next regular meeting;

➤ that the assembling of the agenda will be directed by the CAO with input from department heads; and that the CAO will attempt to brief the agenda committee as to the agenda matters prior to any meeting of council;

➤ that the agenda committee cannot delay consideration of an item referred to it by a committee of council or the CAO any longer than one meeting of council; and

➤ that it is ultimately the CAO's responsibility to check each administrative report being forwarded to council in the context of the following:

- Does this issue need to be decided by council?
- Is this issue of considerable political interest?
- Has the appropriate format been followed?
- Is the information complete?
- Is it well written?
- Do I agree with the recommendation; if yes, have I signed off; if not, have I attached my own report?

With respect to the last point (relative to CAO responsibility), the CAO must ensure that any reports to be presented to council meet his or her standards of quality and completeness. This does not necessitate that the CAO defer or dismiss reports that he or she may not fundamentally agree with; but, rather, requires that the report, along with the CAO's dissenting opinion, be referred to the agenda committee for consideration and possible referral to council.

Chapter 14
Impact of the Mayor

Every mayor has various roles to play in order to be successful. Most of these roles are "common sense" and stem from what is in the legislation or in the literature. The core elements of a mayor's duties are those of any elected member of council. He or she is expected to: represent the electors of the community, as opposed to any individual interests; attend all meetings of council and participate therein; act as a conduit to the administration and obtain information from the CAO; participate generally in the creation or review of policies; and keep matters confidential that are discussed in closed meeting.

The mayor, however, is also expected to: preside at meetings of council; provide guidance to the designated officers; establish committees (or recommend their establishment); provide leadership; and assist in the development of "good government." While not every province calls for each of the foregoing in its legislative description, most would likely ascribe to this general description.

The mayor has considerable power, albeit largely informal, and can exercise this influence over the conduct of the business of the municipality. This does not ignore the fact that the mayor has only one vote on all matters and is, in many respects, coequal with his or her colleagues on council. Rather, it reflects the fact that the public and media often tend to pay more attention to the mayor than to others on council. The mayor must therefore be very prudent in his or her use of this power and exercise it for the good of the community as a whole.

So, What's Missing?

What is often missing is recognition that the mayor can influence the way council conducts its business and shows its leadership style. The mayor, in other words, is not simply "subjected" to the municipality's style of doing business, but rather, should be viewed and understood as a "style master." As such, the mayor should not simply stand by while the CAO or clerk advises as to how the council meeting will unfold; instead, he or she should question why that style is preferred over another.

Much of how council does its business is not in legislation. It is defined by practice. As a result, council might hold a committee meeting with each department head expected to provide a report. Another community might find such a practice offensive, as it runs against the grain of the CAO being the administrative "boss," and thus, no department head reports directly to council. One council might have delegations appear at the start of council business "to get them out of the way," while another might like delegations sitting in chambers a while longer, both to provide an audience (which is how council members get elected) and in recognition that the public *is* their business. One council might set aside a day for the public to appear on a particular issue, whereas another might impose strict time limits and attempt to push public input through a very narrow hose.

These are stylistic issues. They are not the outcome of a strictly prescribed approach to governance (i.e., the only place any of the foregoing is covered in terms of style is in the procedural by-law, which is, after all, the creation of the municipality). Rather, these matters generally reflect the style the municipality has historically applied – and will continue to apply unless someone challenges this *modus operandi*. While new members of council might sit mute as the council meeting unfolds, it will hopefully not be long before one or more enterprising souls (who, after all, were elected as leaders) start to ask questions (i.e., "Why do we do things this way?"). When they hear in reply, "That is what is required by our procedural by-law," hopefully one or more might say, "And why can't we change this?"

Should the CAO and the clerk flank the mayor at the council table? That is what happens in many parts of the country. Where is it writ-

Chapter 14 • Impact of the Mayor

ten? Whoever thought that we should create a seating arrangement that provides for staff members sitting at an elected officials table? Whoever considered that having two staff members sitting on either side of the mayor and whispering into his or her ear during the course of a meeting would not reflect:

- a weak mayor who needs their constant care and attention; or
- a planned disruption and interference to normal discourse between the chief elected official and his or her colleagues?

What are these examples of? Style, personal preference, or, at best, history ("we have always done it this way").

What's missing is leadership. A mayor needs to have an inquiring mind. Why do we do things this way? Who said? Where is it written? Is this the best model? Does council lead, or is it viewed as being led?

If council is THE leadership body of the municipality, is that recognizable? Does it set clear expectations and expect those to be achieved? Does it hold anyone accountable for moving the yardsticks of decision making? Does it sit back and watch others scurry about, setting up agendas and pulling together briefing papers on topics they wish to have approved? How does that activity reflect a council leading?

I would argue that real leadership occurs when council and its mayor actually seize hold of the policy agenda and expect real change. This necessitates a proactive council that engages in constructive thinking – rather than pervasive sitting. It suggests that council might wish to set aside special times for keynote speakers to address the body on key policy topics/themes intended to spark creative thinking, rather than "same old." If the matter is expanding the light rail system into densely populated areas, is that solely an engineering issue, OR should council bring in speakers who postulate on the impact of quality of life indicators? (I am not, by the way, speaking ill of light rail systems as they make good sense from many perspectives. Such systems are not, however, impervious to challenge.) If the matter is that of trying to spark downtown revitalization, should that be delegated to a public committee, or should council host a speakers series wherein creative thinkers and experienced experts are brought to town to address the issue from varied perspectives?

Other than attending a conference of political leaders where some guest speaker might be asked to speak provocatively on the future, what avenues does council have to ensure that the next neighbourhood is actually an improvement over the past? Could it request a report to be commissioned? Why not?

We elect leaders and then we accept (and expect) followers.

Agenda Committee Is Key

In order for the mayor to place council's stamp on the direction of the municipality, it would be ideal if he or she would make use of the agenda committee as a tool or mechanism for doing so. The agenda committee should be charged with overseeing the preparation and content of the agendas for meetings of council. The committee should operate according to strict guidelines, so as not to enable a minority of council members to thwart the will of the majority.

The committee should involve the mayor, plus one at least other council member (the deputy mayor, perhaps), who should offer an oversight perspective, as well as ensuring that the concerns of council are being brought forward. In no instance should such a committee have a quorum of council as its membership. Such a committee will function best with terms of reference, so that no one can manipulate the agenda and restrict issues from being addressed.

Mandate of the Agenda Committee

The mandate of the proposed agenda committee is to ensure that: the business of council is being dealt with fairly and expeditiously; potential agenda items are appropriate for inclusion on an agenda of council and/or committee of the whole; reports from public advisory committees are being received and considered by council; appropriate items are placed on a "consent agenda"; review mechanisms are in place for ensuring that council's committees function effectively as part of the decision-making process; and council is advised as to why any particular matter should not be brought forward for council review at the present time.

Agenda items should include:

- those submitted by the administration (and requiring council's policy review and approval);
- those that council members agree by a resolution of council to place on this agenda for review;
- those that an individual council member might submit, and that the committee believes warrant a report by the administration (and thus, that the committee places before council in the form of a "notice of motion"); and
- those that external boards/agencies have recommended forward to council as their advice on a matter within their jurisdiction.

The agenda committee is not intended to act as a censor for agenda items. Rather, it is to serve as a sounding board for both council and the senior administration to ensure that issues are dealt with effectively and in the proper course of time. The committee is charged with ensuring that the time spent considering council business is used wisely, and that business is conducted as openly as possible, so as to be transparent before the public.

The agenda committee will not have authority to defer any proposed agenda matter for longer than one regularly scheduled meeting without the prior consent of council (by resolution). The director of legislative services will be responsible for establishing a mechanism for tracking these issues and for advising council as to their eventual disposition.

The key determinants of whether or not an issue goes forward to the governance and priorities committee (i.e., committee of the whole as discussed in Chapter 12) meeting should be based on consideration of the following questions:

- Is this a matter requiring council's endorsement?
- Is this a matter for a new or revised policy?
- Does the issue have broad community significance?

- Is this an issue that council might reasonably expect to see and provide direction to, even though it may be within the parameters given to the CAO to act?
- Does the legislation require the resolution of this matter by council?

This proposed model would require that rules of agenda building be developed such that no one abuses the council or committee processes – in terms of resurrecting old issues or otherwise manipulating the content of a council/committee of the whole agenda. It necessitates a structure that places the focus on the truly important issues, and yet ensures that more mundane concerns are at least identified by council and the administration.

Such an approach is designed to ensure that issues are regularly examined from the perspective of "What is the policy issue at stake in this matter?"

Where there is no policy at stake, the following questions need to be asked: "Is it reasonable that we are addressing this issue? Could this not be decided by our administration based on a current policy? If it is not a matter of policy, what is it? If we are a policy body, why are we being faced with such an issue?"

Chapter 15
Role of Standing Committees and ABCs

Effective policy governance can be either aided or inhibited by standing committees and external agencies, boards, and committees. The determining factor as to whether or not committees add value is generally the expectation of the council in establishing or continuing such bodies. What is/was their purpose? Has council received good advice from these committees over the past year? Do they meet regularly? Do they respect the council, to whom the committee reports? Does council invite their chairs to a meeting with council, or can council function for a year and never hear from them?

Purpose of Standing Committees

As noted earlier, standing committees are used by many jurisdictions across Canada for a variety of purposes, but principally to:

- provide policy advice to council on matters within the jurisdiction of the committee;
- provide political input into administrative recommendations at a pre-council stage, so that such input can be considered by council as a whole, in advance of the actual council meeting;
- enable councillors to focus on particular aspects of council business, thereby becoming more familiar with those aspects, and thus more cognizant of the issues and their history;
- provide for a degree of coordination of political issues at a committee stage, to ensure increased corporate integration; and

- increase the awareness of councillors as to the department head (and subordinate) staff, thereby increasing their level of confidence in receiving administrative reports.

There are other purposes for standing committees, to be sure, although the foregoing likely captures the essence of their perceived usefulness. The principal role of such committees should be to provide well-considered policy advice to council, including the analysis of the committee, the options considered, and the rationale for their policy recommendations.

Value of Standing Committees

Standing committees are useful insofar as:

- the terms of reference are broad, rather than narrow (single purpose committees very quickly become administrative in nature);
- the purpose of each is clear (i.e., to advise council *not* to stop members of council from asking questions at a meeting of council);
- such committees report regularly and fully (i.e., written reports are provided to the clerk of council);
- the committees are not used by management to avoid scrutiny by the full council;
- the membership of councillors is rotated regularly, so as to ensure that no one member begins to see himself or herself as a subject matter expert; and
- the committee is reviewed annually to determine if it is still adding value, and thus is useful in its present form.

If council uses a series of standing committees, it needs to re-tool these to be "policy think tanks," rather than rubber-stamping instruments for the administration. Baptizing the CAO's plan on how to address a certain matter is not particularly helpful if that same plan has to come to council for review and approval. Wherein lies the value added? If, however, the CAO frames his or her plan in its policy context and suggests how the policy might be crafted to allow for a new way of addressing the issue, then the subsequent discussion at committee may be helpful.

Standing committees and ABCs (i.e., those created by council) should be expected to adhere to certain governance principles if they are to be retained in this new/revised governance model. Such principles should address: clear purpose statement; terms of reference; advisory role to council; reports vetted by the CAO; committee evaluated annually; council member as liaison only; staff appointed only as advisors; appointments reviewed annually, by mayor; appointments made for no longer than two years; and all committees invited to the annual council "think tank."

Chapter 16
Impact of Administrative Advice

Executive Policy Governance will only be effective insofar as the elected council and its administration fully respect each other and work collegially at making this revised model work. There must be the desire for a clean break: for clarity of roles and respect for one another. The overlapping of council into administrative activities and the administration into governing must become a thing of the past. Council members will understand that they were not elected to manage (regardless of how capable they might have been as managers in their own occupations). The administration, in turn, is delighted that council respects their competency and professionalism, and that council is content to allow its staff to manage within the policies established by council.

Advice to Policy Makers

The potential value added by a well-trained administration lies more in its role of providing good advice to policy makers, than simply as those charged with implementing the decisions of council. Quality advice leads to quality decisions. Thoughtful policies result in well-considered programs and decisions. First-rate advice on all policy decisions of council will be made available to council in writing prior to any such issue being considered. The public will be accorded the best service that the administration can offer. Concerns expressed by the public will be considered seriously and responded to as quickly as possible.

The CAO will work towards the development of a committed management and administrative team, who are able to work collaboratively and share resources effectively. Members of the administration will respect their organization's structure and will ensure that department heads are well briefed, and that the CAO is accorded sufficient information and time to make quality decisions.

Council members need to be reminded that they are not individually responsible for nor entitled to direct any member of the administration. Council (as a corporate body) has one employee – the CAO. It is through the CAO that council as a whole is expected to function. If a member of council is dissatisfied with a response to their inquiry by a staff member, then that concern needs to be taken up with the CAO in a closed meeting of council.

There is also a need for council members to be clear as to which hat they are wearing (i.e., council member or citizen) when they appear at the front counter in the office or any form of electronic communication. Each council member needs to be sure in their own mind whether or not the nature of their inquiry is based on their role as a citizen, a member of council, a real estate agent, a proponent of a charitable organization, a developer, or someone interested in helping out a neighbour who has experienced problems with the municipality.

The moment a citizen is elected, the elected role must supersede any other occupation or position. Such a person can no longer claim to be "just a citizen." In any dealings with the administration, members of council need to act with respect for the roles of the administration. These are not staff of your company or executive assistants to carry out the wishes of individual councillors.

Senior Management Team

Quality governance and leadership depends upon the active presence of first-rate administrators. These people are well schooled and experienced in various settings (normally) and have a well-grounded understanding of the interplay between governance and administration.

While the CAO is recognized by administrators and council members alike as the senior manager, there is also ready recognition of the important roles played by the rest of the senior management team (SMT). The SMT is expected to provide advice to the CAO on all key aspects of the organization, but particularly on any policy issues that will, by their nature, require council approval. The SMT is a central player in the decision-making process by assisting the CAO in preparing and then vetting key reports to council, and ensuring that these reports cover all policy aspects of the issue under review. The team is also instrumental in ensuring that only council-level issues go forward, with the more routine issues being referred back to departments for decisions at that level. Thus, the number and type of items on council agendas should be focused largely on policy matters or essential items (i.e., those that require a council decision).

Role of Administration in Executive Policy Governance

If the new model is given the opportunity to function as intended, it requires that management understand the importance of its own role. Management is principally there to carry out two critical functions:

- ensuring that council is afforded with the best advice possible, based on the competency and experience of the administration; and
- assuring council that its decisions will be implemented expeditiously, respecting the context of council's decision.

Council must be assured that its administration has done everything possible to place quality policy advice before council. This information will have been assembled without any consideration to "How will this fly politically?" The issue of "political acceptability" is not the mandate of the administration; it is the mandate of council. The appropriate research has been done; external advisors have been consulted as necessary; other municipalities may have been consulted; the legal aspects have been checked and verified; and the finance head has been consulted to ensure that the matter is within budget or that the full fiscal consequences have been expressed. At its conclusion, the administration prepares a *policy document* spelling out the best way forward and recognizing that the administrative procedures (i.e., how the policy actually unfolds) will be the responsibility of the administration.

Once any council decision has been made, the task of the CAO and his or her SMT is to get on with the implementation plan. Although council should be kept informed as that plan proceeds, the administration should not ask, "How should we proceed?" If such a question is voiced aloud to council, council will answer; and council members will quickly become embroiled in administrivia. And, the CAO and management will meet privately and ask, "Who thought this was a good idea?" If council demands to see an implementation plan, it will be provided "for information only." If the administration needs such advice from council, they should be encouraged to seek other employment and council should seek those who can (and are willing to) manage.

Chapter 17

Where Does the Public Fit?

Any system of local government that overlooks the role of the public and its right to be involved is unworthy of consideration. Whether it is demonstrators in a public square in the Middle East or aboriginal groups marching in front of the House of Commons, the right of the public to impact its government should never be denied or intentionally relegated.

We are, however, in danger of doing just that: we seem to have become so focused on how we can make governance efficient that we run the risk of seeing it lose its effectiveness. There is no question that governance is cleaner, simpler, and more professional if we just leave it to the politicians and their trusted administrative advisors. The public asks too many questions. They speak out of turn. They mistrust easy answers. They do not accept the first response as necessarily the right one: they suspect that there may be a better one – and sometimes they are right.

Governance, at least at the municipal level, was never intended to be slick, professional, and without controversy. It is described as the "government closest to the people" and any attempt to move it away from the hands of those being governed will not be met quietly. Those who offer themselves as community leaders need to understand that this places them in the proverbial "hot seat." Controversy and council seem to go hand in hand.

So, What Is Reasonable?

To understand what is "reasonable," it is perhaps useful to take a look at what is *not* helpful:

- Placing advertisements in the newspaper or online, requesting citizens to serve on local ABCs (agencies, boards, and committees) and then not providing these same people with a full-scale orientation as to how the system works and their expected roles and value.
- Shepherding all delegations to council at the start of each meeting, so as to get rid of them before the real business meeting begins. The public IS the real business. Without the public, council would be irrelevant. Place the delegations throughout the agenda. Let them see how council conducts a meeting; what rules of procedure are followed; how courtesy prevails.
- Placing members on committees and then not expecting much of the committee. That is insulting, and will not only result in the loss of such people, but will also ensure that they dismiss the relevance of council.
- Putting an advertisement in the paper or online, asking community-minded people to show up and discuss the upcoming budget or business plan without any intention of listening, since the plan is already in final form – and council and the administration simply want to be able to say, "We consulted the public."
- Holding public hearings and then strangling the voice of the public in procedures. If the procedures are cut and dried and the issue is emotional, hold a "town hall meeting" and allow everyone to express themselves, whether they have made proper application to do so or not.

In raising these issues, I hope my intentions will not be misconstrued; be assured that I fully support efforts to involve the public in the decision-making process of council. But, my concern is centered on the following basic questions:

- Is this body or process a good use of people's time?
- Does it add value to the community?
- Could it be made to function better with changes to its terms of reference?
- Is the genuine purpose to hear the views of the public, or is it to baptize previously established ideas or recommendations?

Given the rapid pace of change today, the tools used by councils to aid in the decision-making process have been evolving. Some communities have eliminated the use of standing committees of council and advisory committees; instead, they adopt a public "committee of the whole" approach, wherein council meets "in committee" to discuss issues prior to formally adopting any recommendations in a council meeting. Others have continued the use of a wide variety of committees – in part, because they have not, as of yet, become such a problem that council has decided to review their impact on the operations.

Other councils have instituted *ad hoc* task forces to advise and assist council on very specific issues. Such task forces are generally given a fairly rigorous set of terms of reference, along with a deadline date for reporting and a sunset clause (by which the task force ceases to exist after the adoption of its report by council).

Public advisory committees are often used to deal with broader-range issues that have a greater sense of permanence to them. Such committees might include a combination of members of council and the public, albeit heavily weighted towards public representation. (Quite frankly, I fail to see the need for more than one representative of council on any committee, save those that are comprised of council members only.) Further, public advisory committees should be given fairly broad mandates, and not a narrow focus. The more narrowly streamed such committees are, the more they tend to become managers of the system, rather than policy advisors. It is my view that council does not need more administrators, but rather, community representatives who are expected to provide ongoing policy advice on the big issues.

It should be underlined that there is no one "right" way to handle public input. Each community seems to find its own way in this regard, and the techniques should be based on what best fits the community. Having said that, it is my view that a combination of task forces for specific "stand alone" items and two to three broadly-based policy advisory committees has the most likelihood of success (if the terms of reference are clearly stated and timely).

Use of Social Media

The use of social media was not even a question or a phrase that resonated with anyone when I first began consulting. The world has changed. It is no longer a question of whether or not the public will try to get involved using technology that they find familiar and suitable to their lifestyle, but rather, of how frequently and on what type of topics.

Regardless of the communication tool, there are some key principles to observe:

- One of the primary functions of a council is to communicate to the public on a regular basis: this needs to be done through whatever media is most likely to reach the intended audience.
- Council needs to be open to the public and receive input into the decision-making process. Communication is not simply a matter of council getting the message out: it also needs to be about how residents get their message in.
- Communicating with the public is not a one-way street. To be successful, municipalities should be listening and reviewing feedback from the public. Open communication channels for the public allow them to feel their involvement is having a positive effect on local government and their own standard of living. The right mechanisms must exist to receive and integrate public feedback and allow for the citizens of a municipality to have some input into policies, programs, services, and initiatives in their community.
- Council also needs to be "out there" in the eyes of the public and in attendance at community events wherever possible.
- Ideally, communication practices should be proactive and provide timely information to the public on matters that directly affect their daily lives. Citizens want to know what their council members are planning, how it will affect their lives, and how such decisions are being made.
- Citizens want their elected officials to be transparent and the processes to be an "open book." Reporting truth breeds trust. Withholding crucial information or presenting information in

a way that can be misconstrued or intentionally misinterpreted does not support a healthy relationship between the municipality and the public. Not releasing information or choosing what information to release can be seen by the public as using deceptive and manipulative "spin" tactics.

➤ Public perception sometimes seems to reflect the view that community branding, marketing, and communication is a waste of tax payer money. If council is to commit funds to such functions, it must be able to illustrate "why."

What Is Required?

There are certain key fundamentals that a municipality must include in its quiver of tools relative to ensuring that its communication practices are consistent and telling the story. These tools flow out of the policy perspective that this new model embraces. In order to get the most out of a municipality's resources, each council will need to review the following.

Strategic plan – Where does communication fit in the overall priorities of the municipality? How will our communications align with the values and goals that council has expressed as being important?

Communication strategy and budget – The communication strategy should add meat to the bones of the strategic plan by specifying what actions will follow the lofty goals of the plan, and how communication policy and practices will enable the municipality to better relate to its intended audiences.

In order for the communication strategy to mean anything, and to thus "come alive," the municipality will need to put some money towards its implementation.

Implementation plan – This tactical plan will take the communication strategy and make it much more specific. It highlights the actual steps that the municipality plans to take in the next budget year and the cost of those steps. It details what is to be done in terms of local media, public forums, community roundtables, updating the website, etc. The budget available will help prioritize what strategies to implement and identify tools that need to be developed.

Council has a responsibility to communicate with the public, and this area can be improved moving forward. To achieve such an improvement, each member of council could be encouraged to increase the amount of time spent engaging with the public by attending more community events, responding to emails, and even interacting with the public via social media.

Role of public advisory committees – The role and use of public advisory committees (PACs) has ebbed and flowed over the years. Some are still functioning years after their creation; others are in a form of death throes as the council dithers over whether or not to declare the death final. It is not that PACs are ineffective or could not be re-tooled and made *more* effective. It is largely a matter of neglect. It is that council and its administration (in many instances) have not really reviewed how these advisory bodies are performing, and thus they have become more of a nuisance than an ally to good government.

In an Executive Policy Governance model, such committees could only be deemed to "fit" if their focus is kept primarily (if not exclusively) on policy issues. What does council need to understand from a policy perspective regarding the impact of bike lanes on the environment and the free movement of vehicles? Where should this municipality be placing its focus in terms of helping the community be more active (and thus healthy)? Those are *policy* considerations – not issues requiring involvement in the engineering and works departments.

PACs ought to be aligned with the governance and priorities committee of council. If the GPC is council's only standing committee, then the PACs must ensure that their policy recommendations flow through that committee on their way to council. The reporting process must be clear and consistent and ensure reasonable feedback to citizens serving on the PAC.

This process (based on a clear governance philosophy) will, by necessity, require each municipality to disengage from the usual plethora of external agencies and boards, and focus on the very few that actually impact council's agenda. Thus, I would see perhaps the need for two or three PACs, reflecting what council views as important on the local scene. For instance, a PAC on the environment; a PAC on "active living"; and a PAC on sustainability might provide council with public input (again, from a policy perspective) on its three main areas of focus: environment, leisure, and economic viability. A different community down the road may see the protection of people and property as its main focus, and may create a committee with those terms of reference. The key is to have any such committees aligned with the mandate and priorities of council, so that they act as "feeders" to the policy matrix being embraced by council.

PAC Guidelines

Some PAC guidelines follow:

- ▶ The establishment of any PAC should attract a broad cross-section of the community, and not be limited to specific groups, organizations, or backgrounds.

- ▶ Once first appointed by council, any new members should be appointed by council on the advice of the PAC, preferably with the input of senior administration.

- ▶ Public members should be appointed for a term of up to three years, with a possible two-year extension that should be reviewed annually.

- ▶ Public members should be eligible for re-appointment after a minimum of a one-year absence.

- ▶ No member of council will be named as a member of a PAC, but may attend as an observer. Councillors are not expected to be an advocate for the PAC.

- ▶ Existing special interest bodies (boards and committees) should be expected to report through the PACs to ensure that their concerns are reviewed in a larger context, and to see how they might be streamlined to increase their effectiveness.

- ▶ Unless specifically granted the power to do so, no PAC has the power to pledge the credit of the municipality or commit the municipality to any particular action.

- ▶ The CAO will designate a recording secretary for each PAC (or delegate this responsibility to another member of the administration). Meetings of a PAC shall be recorded in sufficient detail

(including a listing of alternatives considered and costs for any action item) to enable all council members to be reasonably conversant with the action required whenever a report appears before council.
- No member of the public shall give specific direction to any staff member at any PAC meeting. The responsibility for giving specific direction to staff shall reside with the CAO.
- All action items included in meetings of a PAC shall be referred to the CAO for review prior to final consideration by council.
- The CAO will designate which senior staff member is to be the primary linkage to which PAC.
- All management reports going to a PAC will be sent first to the office of the CAO by the respective department head and will be initialed by the CAO to signify that these reports have been seen by the CAO. The CAO shall endorse the report or may wish to submit a separate covering memo to the report, indicating why he or she is unable to endorse it.
- No PAC shall have the authority to establish a sub-committee.

Task Forces

Councils might wish to consider establishing task forces for any future "single issue" problems that council believes warrant the input of the public. Each task force should be:

- governed by written terms of reference prior to council approval of the task force;
- be limited in membership to between five to seven members of the public only;
- composed of a cross-section of those involved with the issue (or as a broader cross-section of the community);
- advisory to a PAC or the governance and priorities committee of council;
- established only by council; and
- including a "sunset clause" in its terms of reference, indicating the date by which its report is due and the date by which the task force will cease to exist.

Chapter 18
Review of Key Concepts

As I begin to draw this series of inter-related thoughts and principles to a close, it might be useful to look back on the key messages.

20 Key Concepts

The following provides a summary of the key, foundational concepts that support the Executive Policy Governance model.

1. Leadership is a scarce and very valuable commodity – Often more known by its absence than its presence, leadership is absolutely critical to the success or failure of organizations. Leaders influence others to move in a particular direction. Leaders can often see a target more clearly and more quickly than others and they have the presence necessary to cause others to move in that desired direction. Leadership is the art of getting others to the preferred destination.

2. If councils are to govern effectively, they must be "released to lead" – The value that council brings to the table is not the combined expertise of all its members but, rather, its capacity to actually lead the community towards its preferred future. How council does this is the key to whether or not it will be successful.

3. Each council has basic, generic responsibilities that flow from legislation, including local charters and by-laws – These responsibilities, while not necessarily common in their interpretation across jurisdictions, are focused on the basic services necessary to ensure the municipality's ongoing ability to function.

4. Each council has a leadership role relative to these basic services – Each council must determine the level of service provided, and thus the degree of funding such services will cost. This determination lies at the heart of civic budgets and drives tax rates and utility charges. Such decisions are not made in isolation: they are considered in light of what council deems to be priorities, both in terms of their urgency, as well as overall importance to the community.

5. Opportunities for failure abound – The number of reasons why elected councils fail in their task of governing effectively is seemingly infinite.

6. Policy governance is not applied consistently across nor within in any given region – This is due, in part, to the fact that what a council is to do is legislated (at least in terms of the greater roles); *how* a council goes about these tasks is left largely to the dictates and preferences of each council. Some have been well trained; some inherit good practices and simply improve those; others access enhanced training opportunities or qualified people.

7. If council is interested in making a lasting difference, it needs a dynamic policy agenda and a refined policy framework – Busyness does not count; attending innumerable meetings matters little; holding positions locally, provincially, and federally may seem important at the time, but that too will be short-lived. What counts is how each council treats the matters of governance that appear before it at every meeting of council, and whether it did so in a consistent, thoughtful, and compassionate manner.

8. Governance style is critical to achieving results – The question might arise: "Why is the governance model (or, in other words, the way by which we do business in council) so important?" The simple response is: "It's important because the model of governance either facilitates or impedes how council does its business." Some councils have struggled with their style of governing, while others have seemingly been able to move forward with much greater ease and results. While that may be partly a result of the personalities elected for each term, the type of community, or the number of big issues with which council is confronted, the mechanisms that council uses to make its decisions also have a significant impact.

9. A new model should be considered – Executive Policy Governance is that model, explained and defined in this book as:

> *The leadership of an organization through the conscious policy choices and decisions made by the executive decision makers (both political and administrative) based on a comprehensive, thoughtful, policy-based framework.*

10. Governance principles are interdependent – The principles that undergird Executive Policy Governance are designed in such a way as to be interdependent.

11. Governance model must be founded upon objectives and design criteria – Council's governance model needs to be designed in such a way that it achieves the objectives as stated, and does so while meeting certain "design criteria." Such criteria might be thought of as "building blocks" upon which the governance model ought to be established.

12. Policy development enhances the effectiveness of both council and the administration – Well-written policies ensure that council need not spend time revisiting routine issues. Instead, the administration has clear direction, founded upon the intent of council, to act and respond in such situations.

13. Separation of roles must be clear and respected – An Executive Policy Governance model is founded upon the clear separation of roles. Such a system only works well if both elected and appointed officials understand their respective parts to be played and refrain from succumbing to the temptation to stray over into the mandate of the other.

14. GPC offers an important forum for non-confrontational discussion of policy issues – The purpose of the governance and priorities committee (GPC) is to enable council members to discuss key agenda issues with the administration in a non-confrontational environment prior to the presentation of such matters as action issues on a council meeting agenda. The GPC is not expected to make any key decisions, as that role should be reserved to a regular meeting of council. The value of a GPC meeting (open to the public) lies in its purpose, which is a forum (for council members and the administration) to present and discuss the more consequential policy issues. These are the issues that have a broader impact on the overall council agenda (i.e., its priorities) and thus should be discussed in a setting that lends itself to discussion, rather than resolution.

15. Council meetings matter – The meetings of council are critical to the decision-making process, as it is at these meetings that final decisions are rendered. As a result, careful thought should be given to their planning, intent, procedures, and follow-up action.

16. A proactive council will seize the policy agenda – Real leadership occurs when a council and its mayor actually seize hold of the policy agenda and expect real change. This necessitates a proactive council that engages in constructive thinking, rather than pervasive sitting.

17. Value of committees will depend on expectations – Effective policy governance can be either aided or inhibited by standing committees and external agencies, boards, and committees. The determining factor as to whether or not committees add value generally depends on the expectations of council in establishing or continuing such bodies.

18. The administration brings value through good advice to policy makers – The value added by a well-trained administration lies more in its potential to provide good advice to the policy makers, rather than simply in its role of implementing the decisions of council.

19. The role of the public is not to be discounted – Any system of local government that overlooks the role of the public and its right to be involved is unworthy of consideration. The right of the public to impact its government should never be denied or intentionally relegated.

20. Leadership policies are central to good governance – All of the foregoing ideas or concepts are interwoven in a system of good governance. Placing the focus on leadership policies forces the distinction of roles to become sharper in focus.

Chapter 19
Drawing the Strings Together

It is my argument that council will be in a position to exercise far more control over the direction of the municipality and the administrative organization if it has a healthy, robust policy framework. It is impossible for an organization to move forward with any degree of confidence if its administrative leadership is constantly looking over its shoulder to see if it is about to be blindsided by the governing council, or if it is expected to explain and defend each and every administrative decision.

There are so many "new" issues that arise in the day-to-day life of a municipality ... the fear that council's involvement will somehow be lessened by the creation of an overarching policy framework is hardly worthy of comment. The council meeting agendas will always be sufficiently crowded with new issues or ongoing controversies, such that asking council to repeat the decision it made last month on essentially the same issue is a colossal (and unnecessary) waste of time and energy.

The public becomes frustrated by the antics of a council that is trying desperately to think of a reason to afford a friend a different solution than that which was determined in essentially the same set of circumstances for someone else a month ago. It makes me wonder why someone from the audience does not cry out, "What's your policy?" when issues are repeated and differing solutions offered. The lack of consistency and "playing everything by ear" reduces the stature of council as quickly as most other foibles (save ethical failures).

To sum up:

- Policies are (or should be) viewed as critical to a competent council.
- A policy framework allows related issues to be reviewed through a broad lens, and not as "one offs."
- Policies are not intended to strangle a council, but rather, to guide it.
- Policies promote administrative surety, consistency, and effectiveness.
- Policies enable public confidence in council.
- Policies are the vibrant, dynamic tools of a confident and competent leadership body.

Leadership and Policy Governance

My basic concern is that elected officials may spend their valuable time at council and committee meetings doing what they think is expected of them, but missing the real object of their leadership roles. We elect leaders to lead; not to place their stamp on decisions that have already been made, or on the actions of other appointed agencies; nor to simply baptize the reports of the administration. Council should be focused on leading – and the way it *does* that is to learn the real value of "strategic thinking" (identifying its goals and priorities) and making decisions count through effective policy governance.

It is impossible to expect council to have its hands on every decision or action undertaken by the administration. The beauty of that "dilemma" is that council does not have to be involved in, or on top of, such decisions: a council can lead very effectively by setting the governance envelope. Council needs to identify the major issues facing the community and determine the answer to a very straightforward (yet not simple) question: What is our policy?

Policies are tremendous instruments of intended action: they direct others to follow the lead of those governing. Without such a policy envelope, organizations drift. With a clear policy perspective, however, municipal organizations can be both effective and efficient.

Best wishes on your governance journey!

MUNICIPAL WORLD PUBLICATIONS

To order any of the following Municipal World publications, contact us at mwadmin@municipalworld.com, 519-633-0031 or 1-888-368-6125, or visit <books.municipalworld.com>.

10 Trends for Smarter Communities (Hume) – Item 0037

Brands Buzz & Going Viral (Chadwick) – Item 0077

Cultural Planning for Creative Communities (Hume) – Item 0035

Deputy Returning Officers Handbook – Item 1280

Digital Connections: Social Media for Municipalities & Municipal Politicians (Chadwick) – Item 0076

Electing Better Politicians: A Citizen's Guide (Bens) – Item 0068

Guide to Good Municipal Governance (Tindal) – Item 0080

Making a Difference: Cuff's Guide for Municipal Leaders Volume 1: A Survival Guide for Elected Officials (Cuff) – Item 0059-1

Making a Difference: Cuff's Guide for Municipal Leaders Volume 2: The Case for Effective Governance (Cuff) – Item 0059-2

Measuring Up: An Evaluation Toolkit for Local Governments (Bens) – Item 0061

Municipal Election Law 2014 – Item 1278

Municipal Ethics Regimes (Levine) – Item 0045

Off the Cuff: A Collection of Writings Volume 1 (Cuff) – Item 0055-1

Off the Cuff: A Collection of Writings Volume 2 (Cuff) – Item 0055-2

Off the Cuff: A Collection of Writings Volume 3 (Cuff) – Item 0055-3

Ontario's Municipal Act – codified consolidation – Item 0010

Ontario's Municipal Conflict of Interest Act: A Handbook (O'Connor/Rust-D'Eye) – Item 0050

Places and Spaces (Hume) – Item 0038

Politically Speaking: Media Relations & Communication Strategies for Municipal Politicians (Chadwick) – Item 0075

Procurement: A Practical Guide for Canada's Elected Municipal Leaders (Chamberland) – Item 0070

Public Sector Performance Measurement: Successful Strategies and Tools (Bens) – Item 0060

Rediscovering the Wealth of Places: A Municipal Cultural Planning Handbook for Canadian Communities (Baeker) – Item 0025

Roadmap to Success: Implementing the Strategic Plan (Plant) – Item 0084

Run & Win: A Guide to Succeeding in Municipal Elections Second Edition (Clarke) – Item 0020

Rural Community Economic Development (Caldwell) – Item 0015

Stepping Up to the Climate Change Challenge (Gardner/Noble) – Item 0095

Strategic Planning for Municipalities: A Users' Guide (Plant) – Item 0085

Taking Back Our Cities (Hume) – Item 0034

The Local Food Revolution (Hume) – Item 0036

Town & Gown: From Conflict to Cooperation (Fox) – Item 0065

Truth Picks: Observations on This Thing Called Life (de Jager) – Item 0090